Paws and Smell the World

Karla Austin, *Director of Operations & Product Development*
Nick Clemente, *Special Consultant*
Barbara Kimmel, *Editor in Chief*
Kara Smith, *Production Supervisor*
Heather Malk, *Production Assistant*
Bill Jonas, *Designer*
Design concept by Amy Jefferson, Whispering Dog Design

Photographs courtesy of Dana Thomas, EdD, compiled from friends and fellow dog lovers

Library of Congress Cataloging-in-Publication Data

Paws and smell the world : unforgettable moments with our best friend / by Dana Thomas.
p. cm.
  ISBN-13: 978-1-933958-28-6
  ISBN-10: 1-933958-28-6
1. Dogs—Literary collections. I. Thomas, Dana, 1962–

PS509.D6P39 2008
810.8'03629772—dc22
                  2008012669

BowTie Press®
A Division of BowTie, Inc.
23172 Plaza Pointe Dr., Ste. 230
Laguna Hills, California 92653

Printed and bound in China
15 14 13 12 11 10 09 08   1 2 3 4 5 6 7 8 9 10

For Otter, Mick, and Montana

"Nobody can ever take a friend's place . . . nobody."
~Maya Angelou

Paws and Smell the World

the World

Unforgettable Moments with Our Best Friend

by Dana Thomas, EdD

Contents

All Paws Forward

We all have high expectations when we bring our new puppy home. We're going to teach him to be the smartest, best, most obedient dog in the world. We already know he's better looking than any other puppy. Now we need to make sure he's better behaved.

We buy armloads of liver treats, "gimme-strips," and beefy biscuits to aid in the training. We purchase books and subscribe to magazines that affirm that we are providing appropriate measures of discipline. We enroll in puppy classes at pet supercenters. We're all about our puppy, and we are blissfully content.

And our puppy learns quickly. He can sit. He can lie down. He can speak. With assistance, he can roll over. And with no other dogs around, he can, for the most part, come when called. And our chests puff out, and we are pleased.

But do we ever stop to consider that, while we pride ourselves in having taught our dogs how to get along in life, it's our dogs who teach *us* the most valuable lessons of all?

This book is not only a celebration of our dogs but also a discovery of the values that our interactions with them teach us. You will recognize all of the situations, whether you have consciously thought about them or not. In some cases, you will believe these vignettes were written about you and your dog.

These stories and poems were composed by dog lovers for dog lovers. I know you will enjoy them. But most important, I hope you learn from them something that will enhance your relationship with your very best friend, your dog.

After all, as Maya Angelou says, "Nobody can ever take a friend's place . . . *nobody*."

Preface

This collection of stories and poems comes from five strong dog advocates who possess the perfect ingredients for rewarding canine companionships: we have a passion for our pups, a keen understanding of who we are in relationship to our dogs, and thoughtful yet confident voices to share the lessons we've learned—all told from our own specially selected points of view.

Much of the prose is personal, some of the vignettes are fiction, and the poetry ranges from silly to serious. But all of the work is intended to bring you one step closer to an authentic friendship with your dog.

If you come away from these readings with anything, may it be a better understanding of how critically important our dogs are for our psyches' total health. I hope that from this book, your soul, your spirit, and your life will be wholly renewed and that you can rekindle a deeper love affair with your dog than you ever knew possible.

There are, of course, those to thank for helping me complete this project:

🐾　🐾　🐾

Laura Kangas, "The Dance," "Spellbound," "Pizza Box Blues," "Grand Theft Frodo": I would never have become the dog lover I am had it not been for my best friend, whose good advice continuously helps me be the best dog guardian I can be and whose complete respect for dogs—*all* dogs—inspired this work from beginning to end.

🐾　🐾　🐾

Amy Jefferson, "My Otter": My wonderfully delirious niece, whose life is complete only with a dog by her side and whose gift as a graphic artist is second only to her virtue as a humanitarian. The untimely loss of her Lab, Otter, during the creation of this book was tragic; her strength to forge ahead, committing to crafting the look of the book, helped seal the vision for this project.

Derrick Jefferson (a.k.a. Ace Winn), performance artist for "Paws and Smell the World": So talented, so giving, the beautiful music he made with my words melts in my ears and brings warm tears to my eyes and shivers to my soul. Thank you for sharing your voice. You can hear this song on my Web site at www.drdanathomas.com.

Rebecca Englert, "Southpaw's in the Ring," "Five Days Stray," "Mama Knows Best": What remarkable writing from this young novice! The power in her stories comes from the passion in her heart for dogs. She is truly the animal advocate, always on a mission to save one dog at a time. She provided the necessary realism and balance for this work.

Mark Smith, "Coconut Harry": More accomplished at writing than he realizes or admits, Mark Smith saved the day with his last-minute contribution to the book. He is a native Floridian, is a singer and songwriter, and is active in the Florida folk music community.

Jacky Sach, agent, Bookends, Inc.: One woman who had perseverance, patience, and belief in this work. Her steadfast determination in publishing this book resulted in finding the best venue for its debut.

Dozer, English Bulldog: My dog and my muse. May I be the person he needs me to be.

Chapter 1

Appreciation:
An expression of thankfulness, admiration, approval, and gratitude

When we're young, we think we have a grip on what is important. The party next Friday, the cool car we drive, the clothes we wear, who we're dating, who likes us, who doesn't. These are defining moments.

Over the years, we learn that other things matter. Quiet time at home on a Saturday night with our loved ones beats the heck out of gallivanting off to the local club to dance until dawn. A solitary walk on the beach in search of a few sun-bleached shells is much more gratifying than braving the crowded, bustling mall to catch a few weekend sales. Working in the garden takes precedence over working late at the office to get ahead.

Sometimes, though, it takes others to help us understand just what we appreciate. And oddly enough, it doesn't have to be a spouse or a sibling, an aging parent or an offspring. It can be—yes—a dog.

A solid dose of appreciation forces our perceptions to do a 180-degree turnaround. We learn that life is something that grows in value—it appreciates. As we appreciate life, we become more valuable—both to ourselves and to others. In fact, learning how to appreciate both the pleasant and the unpleasant and to value each more consistently is a key to increasing fulfillment.

The next few vignettes offer a matchless slant on appreciation. Join Indy the Border Collie in "The Dance," where his performance on the kitchen floor for a few morsels of food leaves his guardian quite reflective. Watch the workplace become an outlet for mothers bursting with pride in "One Up on Dr. Spock," as one dog-mama finds amusement in outwitting her co-workers by comparing her baby to theirs. Identify with those old familiar aphorisms you heard as a child, and chuckle when you realize you're claiming them as your own and loving every minute of it in "If I've Told You Once, I've Told You a Thousand Times . . ."

If you've forgotten how to enjoy the world, or if you've let the daily grind get past you without you noticing, these stories will sketch a map to rediscovery so you'll find yourself saying thanks to your favorite friend—your pup.

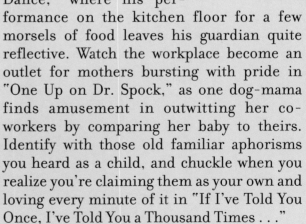

12   Paws and Smell the World

The Dance

by Laura Kangas

My husband and I live with two Border Collies and a Chihuahua in a 1,259 square foot house. We're cramped but happier with three dogs than without.

One of the Border Collies is an older rescue we took in about five years ago. A best guess as to his real age puts him somewhere around eleven to thirteen years old now, as evidenced by the increasing number of gray hairs that outline his eyebrows and snout. He arrived at our house with the name of Indy. We liked it, so we kept it.

Indy has an amazing gift I like to call foodar. Foodar is much like radar, and it is activated only when food (ANY food) is present. The food can be wrapped or unwrapped, raw or cooked, vegetable or meat—it makes no difference; Indy is not a picky eater. At the first sign of any paper rattle, bag rustle, or wrapper cracking, Indy is suddenly *there*. He appears from nowhere— stealthily making his way

Bring out the FOOD, and you have a dance floor.

into the kitchen to stand at my side, his head under my elbow, looking up—waiting, waiting for something, anything, to drop or be handed his way. His persistence usually pays off.

Our kitchen is roughly 100 of our house's 1,259 square feet. It's a small kitchen, big enough only for the requisite kitchen appliances and one human to perform the requisite kitchen duties. Two humans and you definitely have cramped quarters. One human and one fifty-five pound dog and you have a situation that requires extreme agility. Bring out the food, and you have a dance floor. Yes, a dance floor. You see, Indy is persistent—even more persistent in his old age than I recall in previous years. His determination to be in the kitchen with me has become unwavering. Thus, we dance.

I chop brussels sprouts; Indy stands poised on my left, waiting for the minuet to begin. I turn to my right to throw away scraps; Indy

glides to my right. I move to the countertop to chop again; Indy boogies to my left. I step forward to grab something from the cabinet; Indy fox trots back. I pivot 180 degrees to reach for something; Indy performs a grand jeté, turning 180 degrees in the opposite direction. I reach into the fridge for more vegetables; Indy tangos behind me. I chop-chop; he cha-chas. You get the idea. Indy is Fred Astaire, and I am his Ginger Rogers in our 100 square foot kitchen discotheque.

Tip-tap, tip-tap go his toenails as he sashays gracefully over our wooden dance floor like a Gregory Hines hound. This goes on until such time as I notify Indy that remaining in the kitchen is NOT an option—the dance is over; the cancan is now a can't-can't. He hangs his head and pretends to leave. But I know better. He is usually waiting around the corner just long enough so that he thinks I have either forgotten or changed my mind. Then he's back, wanting to waltz yet some more. So I finish my slicing and dicing while he leaps to the left and right, fandangos front and back, and shuffles side to side, a regular danseur noble performing his very own kitchen polka.

Indy is a great dancer—something I will always remember him for and will miss when he's gone. My other dogs have not yet mastered this talent, and I'm not sure I want them to. Dancing is Indy's specialty—his very own trait that makes him unique. The kitchen mambo, the Border Collie two-step, whatever you'd like to call it, these are Indy's very own creations.

And as it turns out, Indy loves raw brussels sprouts.

One Up on Dr. Spock

I'm someone who isn't particularly touchy-feely, so it's never a surprise when I become a little agitated over the obligatory office parties, particularly showers—specifically *baby* showers.

It's not that I don't enjoy baby shower food because I can never get enough of those deliciously sweet petit fours and the triangle-shaped pimento cheese sandwiches. I can even tolerate the silly games of "Name the Baby" that push the usual office drones into tittering giggles. I simply busy myself cleaning up the mounds of pastel pink and blue wrapping paper while the others ooh and aah.

No, I think what I hate most about office baby showers is the aftereffect. Office baby showers propel even mothers of teenagers into months of reminiscing about their own pregnancies, their children's births, war stories about the toddler phase, and those enjoy-them-now-because-they-grow-up-

too-fast warnings. This hoopla is, of course, always reinforced with pictures documenting every stage of metamorphosis: the swaddled newborn, the first tooth, the drooling spaghetti-eating event, the birthday party, the no-training-wheels bike ride. It's just too much.

By now you've probably figured out that I don't have children. That's right. I've never gained weight in my ankles, never taken pride in purchasing "fat clothes," never had labor pains.

Don't get me wrong. It's not sour grapes you're hearing. I'm a mother of a different kind—a mother to three dogs. What you're hearing is the no-frills voice of a dog owner—one who faces mounds of discrimination in the workplace.

When Jessica (mother of two girls) can't come to work for a week because her children have chicken pox, the sympathy wagon rolls in. "Imagine what she's going through!" the secretaries chime. They pitch in their dollars to

I'm a mother of a different kind——a mother to THREE DOGS.

purchase a basket of Aveeno soaps and bath beads. They throw in a bottle of wine for the mom. All I get is a desk full of Jessica's work from her in-box. I wonder what they'd say if I called in to report that my Lab had a skin rash and I had to miss a few days.

My office discrimination is not a hopeless plight. I think I have a solution to my feelings associated with canine-induced employee prejudice. Just imagine these delightful scenarios:

🐾 🐾 🐾

"Laura, great news!" Susan squeals. "Alan and I just got approval from the adoption agency. We're going to be parents!"

"That's great, Susan. You know, you and I have more in common than I thought."

"How's that?"

"Well, Gary and I visited the Humane Society this weekend, and we adopted a beautiful baby Bull Terrier." I flash open my eyes and drop my mouth open in animated glee.

"Ooooooh," Susan blurts with a downward tone. She slithers back to her cubicle. Victory is mine.

🐾 🐾 🐾

"Hi Laura, guess what?" Rachel asks as she passes my desk.

"Yeah?" I say, trying to seem interested but knowing that it's got to be kid-associated, since she's had three babies in three years.

"Carlie rolled over in her crib this morning! It was so amazing! She just—"

"Without a treat?" I interrupt. "Geez, that gal's gotta learn you don't work for free!"

Rachel spins on the heels of her pumps and disappears.

🐾 🐾 🐾

"Joanne, what's that on your suit coat?" I ask.

"Oh, Zack spit up this morning. Poor little darling—"

I tilt my head with understanding. "My puppy chucked on the carpet this morning, too. He's tough, though. Went right back to his food bowl for more chow."

Joanne's forehead creases and her eyes squint. She's definitely more stressed than I am.

🐾 🐾 🐾

"I just got pictures developed of Joey!" Sandra slaps the twenty-four double prints on my desk. "Take a look!"

"Hold on," I beg, digging through my purse. "Check out mine."

"Your nephew?" Sandra asks, knowing I'm thirty-five and childless.

"Dog," I plant the word firmly. "We went to the park this weekend and got some great shots of the Collie playing Frisbee."

Sandra snatches her photos and moves to the next office to showcase Joey.

And it could go on and on all day. I could run with the best of them. I mean, in three years I've literally been through the entire Piaget realm: we've bought teething rings, lost baby teeth, gone to the park, dressed for holidays, taken pictures with Santa, gotten Christmas stockings, taken baths, picked out new toys, had birthday parties, slept through the night, learned to hold our pee-pee, and learned to speak and catch ball.

So, you see, we're no different from traditional families. We just haven't been accepted yet.

I can't ever imagine having this much fun with anyone except my dogs. I've got the best of both worlds—I can experience the wonderful growing pains of raising "children" just as my co-workers do, and along the way I can drive them crazier than they drive me. How cool is that?

Paws and Smell the World

If I've Told You Once, I've Told You a Thousand Times . . .

*I*t's hard being a parent, doing parentlike things, saying parentlike sentences—the kind that make your kids roll their eyes, drop their heads, and walk away. We don't enjoy disciplining our children. We stand firm on the fact that it hurts us more than it hurts them. However, some of the most cliché statements we ever utter are so essential to the bottom-line truth that *not* to say them would be, well, just wrong.

In my house, I rattle off the phrases my mother used on me, and they are probably the same words her mother used with her. The only difference between us is that while they were talking to their children, I'm talking to my dog. And yes, the dog knows the routine: lower the ears, drop the head, and slowly slink to the other side of the house. Pitiful.

It happens without my thinking—this maternal vernacular—and it epitomizes my role as caretaker and controller.

It doesn't take Pavlov to tell me that they learn a LOT MORE QUICKLY than my kids did.

To the kid (dog) who finds pleasure in rolling in the mud: "Get out of the dirt; you're gonna get worms!"

To the kid (dog) who just shredded a four-pack of new toilet paper: "Just look what you've done! That cost me money!"

To the kid (dog) who refuses to come when called: "Do you want a spanking?"

To the kid (dog) who squirms while I wipe dinner from the cheeks (jowls): "Be still while I wipe your face."

To the kid (dog) who is looking rather guilty for digging the two-foot-deep hole near the shed: "I told you not to do that."

To the kid (dog) who returns to the two-foot-deep hole to continue digging until the hole is now three feet deep: "What did I tell you?"

To the kid (dog) who'd rather sit outside during the spring shower than come inside where it's dry: "Come in out of the rain! You're gonna catch your death."

To the kid (dog) who'd rather run through the house and shake the walls than go to the large grassy backyard: "Go outside and play!"

And so the officious instructions continue day after day. In fact, we actually get bossier each week without realizing it. And before we know it, we are maternal dictators, guiding their every move, talking to them more and more, giving them command upon command, and all the while never realizing that—unlike real kids—they never turn fifteen and start with the back-talk. They never turn sixteen and get their driver's licenses and hop in a car and speed away. They never turn seventeen and graduate from high school with goals of getting their "own life." And they never turn eighteen and move out.

They, instead, keep looking at us with those loving, needy eyes. They keep listening to us while we yap at them. They keep silent and give us our say-so. And they never, ever make us feel stupid or dorky or old or unappreciated. They don't even harp about a generation gap. They are—well—wonderful. They empower us.

Sure, they disobey, but they have an excuse because they're dogs, so we don't feel like a failure when they do break the rules. We merely gain strength to try harder to teach them right. And it doesn't take Pavlov to tell me that they learn a lot more quickly than my kids did.

So when I shout "Hush up that barking!" to my pup, he does right away. And I smile. Life is good.

Chapter 2

Simplicity:

Not complex or complicated or involved

If you've ever wished life could be more magnificent, hold that wish. Think about those daily operations of living that we take for granted: sweeping the porch, working in the yard, driving to the office, meeting a new client. We hustle and bustle through each day without considering that every act we perform holds its own set of wonderful nuances. How amazing our lives would be if our hearts raced with anticipation every time we took the weekly trek to the grocer's or if we got giddy over dragging the trash to the curb. How grand the world would appear if we could embrace all that just-waiting-for-us-to-grab-hold-of simplicity.

If dogs were placed in our lives to balance our blasé outlook, then the idea of pairing people and pooches was pure brilliance. Consider the wisdom our dogs possess. Be it a car ride, a neighborhood stroll, or an evening bath, each routine becomes a thrilling world-premiere event, never snubbed for triviality, always approached with frenzied excitement and treated as a significant first-time affair.

In this chapter, aptly titled *Simplicity*, we celebrate our dogs' attitudes toward those occurrences in life that humans very often consider mundane. "Hangin' out the Window Like a Dog, Dog, Dog" offers a dog's-eye view of a road trip to the local fast-food chain and reaffirms how delightful an afternoon  with the top down can be. "Walk This Way" takes the reader on a unique tour around the block, where giving in to the impulses of a leashed dog results in rediscovered childhood memories. Finally, in "Rub a Dub Dub," complex emotions surrounding the dreaded bath result in simple, clean happiness—but not before we realize how momentous the occasion really is for pupster.

All three portraits touch upon something we wish we had more of in our lives: simplicity. They lead us to our admission that we don't stop to smell the roses often enough. And they comment upon what our dogs already do naturally: pause and smell the world.

Paws and Smell the World

Hangin' out the Window Like a Dog, Dog, Dog

Ah, what a feeling! It's a beautiful, cloudless March afternoon, the top is down on the convertible, and a cool wind is blowing through my hair, er, fur.

I'm joyriding, being chauffeured in style. Got no particular destination and couldn't care less. If I could muster a bark in tune, I'd sing "Feelin' Groovy."

I spring to the passenger door's ledge and stretch my neck high. A few deep sniffs of country breeze and pure bliss envelops my being. I drop my jaw and out flaps the longest tongue in the world. The swift air catches it, and it ripples like a flag at full post.

The car accelerates, and my muscular hind legs bump the back of the seat. I spread my front paws wide to steady myself. My chauffeur places her hand on my hips to ensure I don't bolt. I close my eyes and imagine how it would feel to leap like a flying squirrel, be caught in the swirl of currents, and

I DROP my jaw and out flaps the longest tongue in the world.

land in the soft pile of green that borders the road.

I open my eyes, swivel toward the most beautiful driver in the world, and pull in my tongue out of courtesy. She returns the gaze and pats me on the head.

She begins the usual round of nonsensical questions—a mere formality, nonetheless part of the event. My attention to her words makes her happy, so I play along.

"Do you wanna go on a car ride?" she asks in a soprano voice.

I wiggle my tail (that means yes). I'd like to inform her that we already *are* going but don't want to insult her, so I wiggle my tail again, this time more quickly. This action only encourages the conversation, and she fires off her second round of inquiries.

"Do you? Do you? Do you wanna go?"

My wiggling is out of control now, and my entire rump is swaying left and

right. She changes gears, and I find myself on the floorboard.

"You love to go on a car ride, don't you?"

Overkill, but OK, I can deal. I jump back onto the passenger seat.

"Don't you?" she asks one more time.

This is my final cue. I offer a crisp, resounding bark. She smiles, satisfied that I'm happy.

She whips into a corner gas station and pumps some super unleaded into the tank. This pit stop gives me time to sample each and every seat in the car. Like Little Red Riding Hood, I turn on my discriminating taste: the left rear seat is too low (prohibits visibility); the right rear has some books

piled on it (I might topple); the middle rear provides no standing support and little wind rush; the front driver's seat is, well, taken. That leaves the front passenger seat—grand view, great air, occasional pats and scratches.

Other people are gassing up, and they smile when they see me. They approach the car grinning at me (I'm *so* cute), they ask if I bite (I don't), and then they begin to stroke my back (one perk to gas-guzzling cars—frequent fill-ups mean attention).

Soon, we're on the road again. Just when we get up to maximum speed—the kind where my ears are peeled back and my teeth are getting wind burned—we come to a squealing stop right beside a small truck. Up from the flatbed pops a rather dopey-looking dog, some type of mixed mutt that breaks every rule in the book of dog breeding. He yelps an irritating "What are you looking at?" and rushes up and down the length of the truck's rear. I bark back, "*You*, Ugly."

Not soon enough, we're moving again and have left the truck far behind. I give a glance over my shoulder, and the wind catches my upper lip, forming a most appropriate sneer in the loser dog's direction.

Suddenly the most overwhelming smell smacks me right in the nostrils. My head involuntarily points skyward trying to capture a lungful of the thick, meaty scent. We pull up to a lighted panel, and a voice from nowhere asks, "May I take your order?"

A few verbal and monetary exchanges later, there sits a white sack of the most wonderful smelling something on the dashboard. I'm torn! What to do? Sit tight and smell the flavor in the bag or stand tall and smell the world? I opt for the former, unable to deny my true love: food. I sit patiently, and she finally dips into the bag and throws a french fry my way.

A double bump over the driveway, and we're home (so soon?). She hops out and moves to my side of the car. She opens the door. I am still sitting. She thinks I want another nibble of her lunch. Truth be told, I'd opt for another race around the block. I mean, who doesn't love a good car ride?

The simple things are what life's all about—the jingle of a set of keys, the rev of an engine, and the hum of an automatic window as it smoothly drops down and out of sight. How sweet the sounds. Let's cruise.

Paws and Smell the World

Walk This Way

My puppy took me for a walk today. OK, I know it's supposed to be the other way around, but if I'm going to be honest, it's not. Could you resist a headstrong pup who takes control of his own schedule? He knows precisely where he wants to go and when he wants to go there, and he has no problem telling me the plans.

The dog's got no need for a Day-Timer; he's got an internal clock that screams Walk Man! The ritual goes something like this: Struts to the front door and barks once. Figures out that I'm not moving. Finds the leash and drags it to my armchair. Drops it at my feet. Steps into his own harness. Waits for the click of the buckle. Heads for the great outdoors. He's eleven months old, and he already knows exactly how to play me.

I can't complain; the dog keeps me on track. He ensures that my life stays on his schedule, and he keeps it provocatively

Our walk had been a journey of SIMPLICITY rediscovered.

simple. The puppy is the reason I get up at a decent hour on the weekends; he's why I opt out of the all-guy spring break fishing trip. He's responsible for me still being able to throw a ball with any accuracy; and, yes, the dog is the motivation I need to put in a good half-mile walk each afternoon.

Today was his entire fault—all his wonderful, wacky fault—and I haven't felt this free in years.

The leash-gathering ritual began at 8:30 a.m., a bit early, as I still had a second cup of coffee to down. But I obliged, seeing as it was a bright, beautiful Sunday morning in April. So off we went, with aspirations (mine) of swiftly covering the block in less than twenty minutes. I'd be back home before *Meet the Press*, and I'd still have time to shower and beat the other shoppers to the grocery-store rush hour.

The problems started at the intersection of the first turnoff. Max wanted to go left—into the woods. We usually go right, down another street of homes.

What the heck, I countered myself. Give him a thrill for once. He never gets what he really wants. Left we turned.

Fifty feet ahead we met up with a ditch. Not an ordinary "Skip-to-My-Lou" ditch, but a you-better-have-waterproof-combat-shoes-on ditch. Max looked over his shoulder, daring me, taunting me with that you-are-a-complete-wuss accusation. I cleared my throat, took a deep breath, and became Carl Lewis going for his final long jump gold medal. My feet shwumped into the mud, and the pull of Max's leash saved me from an instant quicksand suck down.

Suddenly I was twelve years old again and traipsing through the wooded lot next to my childhood home. I prayed that my mother wouldn't see me and hoped that my friends would. I was Timmy and he was Lassie—er—Laddie; I was Johnny Quest and he was my Bandit; I was Shaggy and he was my Scooby Doo, and, boy, we were on to something big.

We neared another trough, this time larger in width and definitely deeper. We peered over the drop-off into the mush, and my stomach did a somersault. Max was ready to plunge down into the thick dollarweed-covered ravine until I pulled back on the lead with a mighty yank. We weren't going there, I insisted, but Max barked a rebuttal, and I reluctantly gave in.

I wouldn't have batted an eye fifty years ago. Where was my desire for simple exploration? Now I blinked once and halfheartedly welcomed the challenge, a stupid grin covering my face. I was a mass of conflicting emotions. Thank God, Max was in charge.

"OK," I consented, in the singsong kind of voice I use when offering Max a treat. Off he trotted while I blindly followed. The leash became our lifeline, our umbilical cord. We were tandem. It was Max who was the guide now, and I was at his mercy. With every dip and turn my heartbeat increased, somewhat from the thrill of exploration, mostly from being out

of shape. My panting drowned out Max's, but soon I was leading, telling Max "come, boy!" not knowing where we were going, but happy to be getting there.

I found myself searching for the perfect stick—something to scatter the crunchy fallen leaves with, maybe uncover a treasure, maybe show this forest who was boss. Max stumbled upon a crooked piece of birch and immediately began to bite it. I issued a frantic "No!" and snatched it up with my free hand. I had found my perfect walking stick.

With each new step, I swiped the branch from left to right and back again with the same rhythm and direction of Max's trot. The staccato pattern calmed my senses and became my compass. Between Max and the stick, I knew I was not lost, only misguided, and that a 180-degree pivot would take me right back to where we started.

A few more yards and the stick caught a root. Thrown off balance, down I went face first in the dirt and leaves. I lifted my head and opened my eyes to discover that what I thought was a twig in my brow was actually the body of an old camouflaged GI Joe. The brittle plastic arms were poised with a rifle, ready to fire at my right eyeball. I blinked two or three times to clear the sand from my rims, and for a few wistful moments I really was twelve and in the mighty throes of war, crawling on my belly, holding my breath, daring the crackle of a brittle twig to expose my location and signal my buddies to begin the barrage of dirt bombs.

Max galloped up and with a few sticky licks encouraged me to get up off the forest floor. I gathered my composure and lumbered forward but was halted by a thirty-pound canine anchor. Max wasn't budging any deeper into the woods. He'd had enough.

I glanced at my watch and realized we'd been gone for over an hour. Perhaps that was why I had to drag Max home. The last fifty feet were merciless on my poor short-legged pup.

He collapsed on the kitchen's cold tile the minute we landed inside. I think he was actually glad to see me turn on the tube and sit down.

Later that day, I rushed to get the leash and approached Max who was spread eagle on the wooden floor of the family room. His tired meter—the tip of his pink tongue—peeked out from his underbite.

"Wanna go on a walk?" I asked Max.

Only his eyes pivoted my way. *You gotta be kidding*, his expression begged.

I squatted and gave him a pat on the head. "Thank you, little guy."

For me, the walk was a journey of simplicity rediscovered. Sure, I didn't balance the checkbook, didn't get Saturday night's dishes put away, and didn't bother to conquer the usual weekend wash-the-car routine. In fact, absolutely nothing on the to-do list got done. But a soul that was missing was found—in the woods, by a dog, who knew where one was hidden.

Paws and Smell the World

Rub a Dub Dub

One dog in a tub.

Stinking, filthy, rotten dog.
Head-hanging, guilt-giving, sticky-mouthed
    dog.
Slobbery, gummy, dirt-ridden dog.
Cowering, slinky-tailed, dramatic dog.
Sand-spurred, muddy-toed, difficult dog.
Inconvenienced, upset, why-do-this dog.
Unappreciative, indignant,
scummy-butt dog.
Stank, rank, sour-smelling dog.
Grimy-nailed, nasty, wrinkled, garbage-
    pawed dog.
Grungy, greasy, get-off-the-carpet dog.
If-you-wash-me-one-more-time-I'm-
    gonna-die dog.
Flea-infested, spit-encrusted, grubby-
    soiled dog.
Foul-breathed, toilet-licking, scratching,
    itching dog.
Giving up, giving in, getting washed dog.

Sprinkled, sprayed, water-backed dog.
Jet-streamed, wet-furred, hosed-down dog.
Dampened, miserable, soggy-eared dog.
Dripping, desperate, let-me-go dog.
Squirted, squirming, want-to-shake dog.

Soaped-up, lathered, scrubbed-skin dog.
Head-turning, pulling back, defiant dog.
Bubbly, foam-covered, frothy-faced dog.
Final-rinsed, doused well, gray-water dog.
Wash-clothed, ear-rubbed, tooth-brushed dog.
Towel-dried, nail-clipped, stiff-brushed dog.

Shiny, soft-haired, frisky dog.
Pretty, proud, show-off dog.
Tearing out, energized, run-the-rounds dog.
Darting, playful, blissful dog.

The if-you-WASH-me-one-more-time-
I'm-gonna-die dog.

Rolling, barking, glad-it's-over dog.
Jumping, thankful, feels-good dog.
No-more-baths-for-two-weeks dog.
I-deserve-a-good-treat dog.
Crunching, munching, relieved dog.
Happy, carefree, relaxed dog.

Panting, slowing, tired dog.
Dropping, lying, resting dog.
Snoozing, snoring, dreaming dog.
Running-through-the-mud-flats dog.
Chasing-squirrels-through-ditches dog.
Getting-stuck-in-swamp-grass dog.
Good-dream-turns-to-nightmare dog.
Owner grabs his dirty dog.

One dog in a tub.

Chapter 3

Guilt:

Justly responsible for a usually grave breach of conduct

One thing we dog guardians want is a clear conscience when it comes to our canine pals. We want to puff out our chests and take pride knowing that Rover—our Rover—is clean, well fed, exercised, healthy, and happy. We also believe it wouldn't hurt if all the other Rovers in the world were the same. And we often like to take credit for contributing to the well-being of dogs in general.

What happens when things *don't* go the way we'd like for dogs is the message of this chapter, entitled *Guilt*. When dogs have bad moments or bad days—or bad lives, for that matter—it isn't always our fault. They may have escaped through the hole they dug underneath the backyard fence; they may have eaten a poisonous bug; perhaps they were born a wild hound in a damp, dark alley. But despite circumstances beyond our control, our bones ache with guilt—that tremendously overriding feeling that leaves us empty except for the piercing black hole in our soul. When situations go wrong with dogs, guilt talks to us, whether we're looking into their crestfallen faces or sitting at the office staring at one of their fifteen pictures pinned to

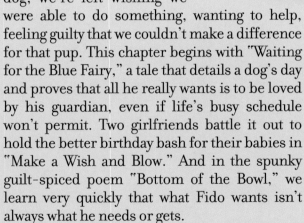

the corkboard beside our computer. When we stumble upon an Internet news story involving the tough luck of a dog, we're left wishing we were able to do something, wanting to help, feeling guilty that we couldn't make a difference for that pup. This chapter begins with "Waiting for the Blue Fairy," a tale that details a dog's day and proves that all he really wants is to be loved by his guardian, even if life's busy schedule won't permit. Two girlfriends battle it out to hold the better birthday bash for their babies in "Make a Wish and Blow." And in the spunky guilt-spiced poem "Bottom of the Bowl," we learn very quickly that what Fido wants isn't always what he needs or gets.

In many ways guilt enables us to come to terms with a reality that might merely have knocked on our doors but never entered. Guilt grounds us in truth; it helps us actively search for creative reactions to issues that may never have a solution but are worth the effort to try and find one. And for all of our thinking, feeling, and trying, our dogs are better off, and so are we.

Paws and Smell the World

Waiting for the Blue Fairy

*I*n Stephen Spielberg's futuristic fairy film *A.I. Artificial Intelligence*, David, a highly advanced robotic boy, wishes to become a real boy so he can win back the affection of the human mother, Monica, who abandoned him. Like Pinocchio, he goes on a long journey hoping to find his Blue Fairy, someone who can make his dreams come true. When he locates her, he sits patiently in an underwater hub for 2,000 years waiting for the Blue Fairy to move, to nod her head, to give him a sign that all will be well. David exhibits dedication, true love, and most of all, patience.

I have become the combo version of the two females in the movie. My dog, an English bully pup named Dozer, is the canine version of David. I am his "mother." He is an only dog—and my first, after forty years of never having successfully gotten past six weeks of dog-rearing (that is another story). Dozer's number-

Worrying is a LARGE part of the contemporary dog owner's psyche.

one goal in life is to love and be loved by me. To accomplish this goal, he waits for me—his very own Blue Fairy.

All that waiting gives me a guilty conscience, something I could not have fathomed a few years ago. Sure, I used to feel bad about leaving my kids with the babysitter on a Saturday afternoon to get the gray in my hair colored, but guilt over my dog? No way! Think again. As the children got older, my guilt disappeared. As Dozer gets older, my guilt becomes more intense. My kids get excited now when I tell them their father and I have a "date." The dog, on the other hand, slinks to his bed, hangs his head, and requires heavy doses of doggy Prozac.

In reality, that's why we dog owners feel a constant pang of guilt. We are all the proverbial Blue Fairy, and we know our pups are doing what they do best: waiting—on us. Think about it. On any given day, well, they simply wait. I mean, look at Dozer's schedule:

6:30 a.m.	Waits for me to wake up
6:45 a.m.	Waits for me to let him out for a potty break
7:00 a.m.	Waits for me to exit the shower, get dressed, and dry my hair
7:15 a.m.	Waits for me to fill his food and water bowls
7:20 a.m.	Waits for me to put the baby gates up in the kitchen
7:25 a.m.	Waits in his bed in the kitchen until I say good-bye
7:30 a.m.–4:45 p.m.	Waits and waits and waits for my return
4:45 p.m.	Waits to be let outside
5:00 p.m.	Waits for me to feed him his dinner
5:15 p.m.–6:30 p.m.	Waits for me to finish my dinner so I'll consider giving him some scraps
6:45 p.m.	Waits to go out after dinner
7:00 p.m.	Waits to be played with
7:30 p.m.	Waits to be played with more
8:00 p.m.	Waits to be played with again
8:30 p.m.	Waits for a taste of my evening snack
9:00 p.m.	Waits to go out for a final potty break
9:30 p.m.	Waits for me to go to bed so he can go to bed

The weekend complicates matters even more. Saturday and Sunday can include, but are not limited to, waiting for a morning walk around the neighborhood; waiting to go to the puppy park; waiting for a trip to the pet store; waiting for the weekend grill fest, where good smells and fat scraps can be had; and, finally, waiting (without glee) for the dreaded bath.

So dogs wait and wait, and we should at least appreciate their patience. Some are better at waiting than others, but we must ultimately remember that in the long run, they are dependent on us. They rely on us for food, water, love and affection, visits to the vet and the park, and that blissful outside time.

Authentic dog ownership is a huge responsibility but one of the most rewarding. While we must wait almost thirty years for our children (whom we *birthed*!) to acknowledge their gratitude to us for taking care of them—the food, the shelter, the everything—our dogs' gratitude is instant and begins at that very receiving-blanket minute. One small scratch behind the ear, one tiny treat, one soft toss of a ball, one little 'atta boy and a dog's loyalty is locked into place for eternity. Tail wags, feet licks, and that I-will-love-you-forever look is enough to make it all worthwhile.

In fact, all that waiting is good for something. Know that Rover isn't just a blankly bored dummy. He's thinking about the future: the car ride to the Frisbee park, the Sunday afternoon walk, the brushing-of-the-dog ceremony after the (yikes) bath. Waiting does pay off.

Of course, we're nothing like the real Blue Fairy from *A.I.* We're not made of stone or heartless and nonresponsive, frozen in time for two millennia. We go to work each morning, and we worry (something I had no idea I would do—I mean, come on! Years ago, I would have argued "They're just dogs!" Wrong!).

Worrying is a large part of the contemporary dog owner's psyche and adds to our stress levels. In fact, on the anxiety scale, I place worrying about Dozer right below being fired from a job and above getting a divorce. We wonder if our doggies are depressed, we hope they're not too cold or hot, and we ask ourselves over and over if we remembered to fill the water bowl. When we get home in the evenings, we drop our keys and take care of their needs before ours. We squeal their names in unnatural octaves to get a rise out of them. We spend our last eight bucks on a nail trim for them rather than a manicure for ourselves. We delight in their delight.

So hey all you Blue Fairies out there, sit up and take notice. Don't make them wait 2,000 years, which, by the way, equals 14,000 years in a dog's life. When we go to sleep with our dogs' warm bodies at the foot of our beds, know that we are their happiness. We are their Blue Fairies come true. What an honor.

Make a Wish and Blow

I dialed my best girlfriend's phone number. When she answered, an involuntary, interrogatory gloat came out of my mouth.

"Guess what *we* just did for the puppy's birthday?" I didn't mean to sound so pompous, but this was my best show of devotion yet to my beloved one-year-old dog. I had definitely outdone myself.

Her reply was rather nonchalant. "What?"

"Well, first I went to the pet supermarket and bought him a new bed. He's outgrown his other one. I picked up some new squeaky toys, too. And a tennis ball combo set."

"That's great," she said. "Actually, my dog needs a new bed."

"Wanna know what else?"

"Sure."

"This is so cool," I added bouncing with pride as I spoke. "I went to the grocery store, and I bought a sheet cake—vanilla, of course. I had

A few candles, a little cake, maybe a new collar, and just US.

the bakers put little paw prints and bones on it. It said Happy Birthday with his name underneath."

"Did you guys eat it?"

"After we sang 'Happy Birthday' and blew out the candles."

"You're kidding, right?"

"No, why would I be?"

"Let me guess," she said. "You had birthday hats and noisemakers and—"

"Of course," I said rather defensively. "If you don't believe me, I have the pictures to prove it."

"Did you rent a clown?" she then asked sarcastically.

"No, he doesn't like clowns. They frighten him."

I sensed a little hostility at the other end of the line and could imagine her rolling her eyes. Maybe she was upset because I hadn't invited her over for the festivities. I thought it would be a bit too much with her three dogs in tow: not enough cake to go around and fights over the new toys.

A huge sigh shot into my ear, followed by her accusatory words. "Well, that's it. I'm a loser.

"Huh?"

"I've had dogs all my life. I've never had a birthday bash for them. Never. You own this dog for nine months, and you're the party planner queen. I'll never live this down."

"Who knows? It's not like I put an ad out in the paper in the social happenings section—although that did cross my mind. And I don't think my dog is going to tell your dogs. Besides, you know that turning one is a big event."

The next week I got a large multicolored envelope in the mail. When I opened it, a handful of glitter in the shape of Mexican sombreros dropped into my lap. It was an invitation to a furry fiesta. "Frodo is turning two!" it announced. "Come celebrate Chihuahua style!" The party was scheduled on Cinco de Mayo and offered puppy piñatas and lamb-and-rice-filled taquitos.

The party was spectacular. My friend had hired a Spanish singing trio, and the canine guests each got complimentary ponchos. It was a veritable dog party extravaganza.

Of course, once the party got going, the guests got a bit wild, and the human hors d'oeuvres toppled onto the ground. In an instant, the pup posse surrounded the food and started crunching tortilla chips. The trio broke into a chorus of "La Cucaracha," and my friend announced it was time to open gifts.

I didn't think to bring a gift. I assumed the host family would provide the new toys and leashes and sweaters and chewies for the honored Frodo. An hour later, we were swimming in shredded wrapping paper, and I had to sweep my dog's mouth to get the wad of gift wrap from the back of his throat. We left shortly afterward, having had just about all the puppy party we could stand.

I have eleven short months to plan for my dog's two-year-old birthday party. I've considered having a tucks-n-tails formal bash complete with bone ties and top hats, concluding in a limo ride to the puppy park, but I know better. My dog likes quality family time on his very special day. A few candles, a little cake, maybe a new collar, and just us egging him on to make a wish and blow.

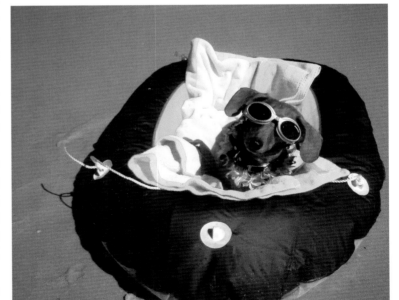

Bottom of the Bowl

Starts from a bag. Cereal slag.
Plywood bits make me gag.
Fifty-pound pile upsets my bile.
It's gonna stay on that plate for a while.

Soy bean, oatmeal, barley, or wheat
Cannot replace that tasty meat.
Dry dog food that has no gravy?
Feed it to the US Navy.

I wanna boycott if it's not
Moist and meaty and sticks to my chops.
I need a fine meal that finds my soul.
Every dog's goal: bottom of the bowl.

Comes from a can. Spoon and shove.
Real meat portions I do love.
Chunks and slices—a canine wish.
Drop it on down into my dish.

Frantic feeding. Jaws go snap.
Teeth are flashin'. Good eats are on
the map.
Tails are waggin'. Long tongues lap.
A dog'll stay home for a
guaranteed snack.

Will not stop till I convince you how to shop.
Moist meaty slop will fill my belly till I drop.
If you understand my craving, then
you've justified your role.
Every dog's goal: bottom of the bowl.

Comes from a grill. Now you're talking.
A dog'll stop dead in his tracks instead
of walking.
He'll remember all his manners like a
Eukanuba champ.

If you understand MY CRAVING, then you've
justified your role.

It's feeling like a home and not a Navy
boot camp.

Smell that meat. Bones tonight.
People-food passion. A dog's delight.
Leftover scraps. The bar-be-que is cold.
Under-table handouts. Fido's gold.

From a bag to a can to a grill—what a toll.
Every dog's goal: bottom of the bowl.

Chapter 4

Love:

Something that elicits deep interest, tender affection, compassion, and enthusiasm in somebody

Ah, sweet love! That wonderful feeling that hits us deep and strong where it counts—in our souls! Those who are fortunate find love at every turn in life, while others often wait an eternity and never find it at all. Want to know a secret? A dog can help you find love in a moment. An initial stroke of soft puppy fur, a first slobbery lick, and one enthusiastic bark will find you a willing slave to the love of a canine cupid.

Luckily, those who place their delight in their dogs find love each and every day. Dogs—loyal, trustworthy, and engrossed in our actions and moods—have an incredible talent for bringing out the best in us— genuine love.

In this chapter titled *Love*, discover the perfect day in the eyes of a dog in the heartfelt story called "What a Dog Wants." Get a hungry, honky-tonk dose of love sickness in "Ode to a Bar-Be-Que," and uncover the secret of why women sometimes jokingly prefer their dogs to their husbands in "All Dogs Really Do Go to Heaven."

While a dog's physical framework and speech may not have commonalities with humans—four legs, fur, tails, and barks— their souls are connected to ours with one of the most basic yet important characteristics in life. Their love for us (and ours for them) transcends us to a higher state, a better, more peaceful condition. Ain't love grand?

Paws and Smell the World

What a Dog Wants

Go ahead. Ask me. Make my jowls curl up over my teeth in a wide, slick smile. Ask me what I really want. And once I tell you, follow through.

Promise?

Alright, I warned you. The list is long, but boy, oh, boy, this is gonna be great.

1. Let's get up with the sun. I love the yard when it's still got a fresh blanket of dew and the crickets are still chirping. The day isn't boiling yet, and if I'm really quiet, I can catch view of a few rabbits and squirrels finishing up their predawn chores.

2. Brush me on the deck. I'm itchy from the past night's sleep and need a good rub to get my blood flowing.

3. Play ball! I know you haven't had your coffee, but I'm full of energy. A little game of hide-and-chase is good for the heart.

4. Time for breakfast. I'd enjoy the scraps from your eggs and toast—feel free to mix it right in with my dry food. You won't see me complain.

5. A zip around the block sounds timely. I'll lead, you follow. Let me stop when and where I want without that ever-annoying yank from your end. I've got things to smell!

6. Back to the house for a little mid-morning nap, please. I'm tired and need my beauty sleep.

7. The stores are cranking and the pet store calls. Socialization is important, remember? Let's pick up a few new squeak chews while we're there.

8. Since we're out, let's hit the puppy park. Don't worry, I won't last long—it's mid-July.

9. To the house! I'm hot and dirty, and although I pretend I don't like baths, well . . . there's something rather appealing about a cool rinse right about now.

10. I'm frisky! And I wouldn't particularly mind a good game of tug with the old rope.

There's nothing like an after-dinner STROLL to settle a meal.

11. Did someone say "afternoon snack"? A smoked pig ear sounds mouthwatering.

12. Zzzzzzzzzzzzzzzz.

13. Zzzzzzzzzzzzzzzz.

14. Dinner is served. Could you mix some fat scraps with the regular chow, please? I'll be your best friend.

15. Walk number two. There's nothing like an after-dinner stroll to settle a meal.

16. The last hurrah. A few games of nighttime chase through the house followed by a nightcap of some biscuits, and I'll be ready to crash in my bed. Sweet dreams.

So, there you go: my idea of the perfect puppy agenda. Try it for one day, and I'll love you for the rest of my life.

Ode to a Bar-be-que

*U*p I jump into the red Ford truck,
Kick back in the bed and wag my
tail for luck.

It's grillin' time and the winds are high.
I just wanna do an afternoon drive-by.

Please head toward the barbeque hut.
I'm proud to be an old meat-
smellin' mutt.

Sure I'm devoted, and I do love you,
But nothing can compare to a doggy
bar-be-que.

T-bone, prime rib, tenderloin, New York
strip,
London broil, leg 'o lamb, filet mignon,
sirloin tip.

Slow down, Mac. Here we are.
The rib shack's ahead. It's not too far.
The smoke stack's streaming; my nostrils
flare.
Can't get enough of that grill-fired air.

I'd really lick my chops for an
outside cut,

But I'll settle for the bone 'cause I know
what's what.

I've given my attention to many
leather shoes,
But nothing can compare to a doggy bar-
be-que.

Rump roast, rib eye, bottom round, beef
flank,
Porterhouse, brisket whole, iron bound,
meat shank.

I'm a HUNGRY HOUND with a sweet
tooth for meat.

It's gettin' dark; it's gettin' late.
Come on out. Have you cleaned your plate?

I'm sleepin' in the truck, tryin' to be
discreet,
But I'm a hungry hound with a sweet tooth
for meat.

Doggy bags can be a mutt's best friend,
Yet the smell in the bag outweighs the taste
in the end.

I told you once before, vegetarians are few,
'Cause nothing can compare to a doggy
bar-be-que.

Chuck eye cuts, delmonico slabs, short loin
shoulder, beef on a rack,
Stir fry nuggets, baby backs, cut beef jerky,
pot roast stack.

I wish I could mature and get a meat-
lover's clue,
But devourin' so quickly leaves me
meatless and blue.

There's only one reason I repeat the
drill anew.
It's the simple fact that nothing's like a
doggy bar-be-que.

All Dogs Really Do Go to Heaven

If you're married and have a dog, then you know this: if your husband and your dog both died on the same day, your dog would be granted entrance to heaven before your husband. That's right. Your dog.

I have experienced my husband's insulting verbosity throughout my marriage. He has commented with a smirk—when he shouldn't—putting himself in the marital dog house. Take, for instance, my night last week:

"Honey, dinner's ready."

"What are we eating?"

"Meat loaf and macaroni and cheese."

"Again? We just had that last week."

"Ground beef was on sale."

"Hope it's not spoiled."

"So eat the macaroni instead."

"You know I've been on a low-carb diet. Geez, you're not helping much."

You see, if I'd been having that conver-sation with my dog, it would have gone something like this:

"Come eat your dinner."

"I'm coming! Oh boy! I'm starved. I can't wait!"

"Here's your puppy chowie."

"I love this stuff! I'll never get tired of it!"

"I'm glad it's on sale this week. You sure go through a lot of it."

"I'd eat anything you gave me! I love food."

"You're getting fat, pup."

"All for you! Feed me!"

Don't misunderstand me. I love my husband, but I absolutely ADORE my furry cherub

Angels. That's what they are. They're sprouting wings and sporting halos minute by minute. I could never tell my husband this, though. He'd be just about as understanding as he was last week during the blanket incident, another one of our he's-got-to-comment episode:

"Where is our old comforter that used to be on the bed?"

"I bought a new one."

"Why? There was nothing wrong with the old one."

"It didn't match."

"And this ugly one does?"

"This one's better quality."

"It looks like it'll be hot."

"So sleep on the couch."

"Fine. You can sleep with the dog."

A dog, however, would have been ever-so-appreciative:

"Oh boy! She bought me a new blanket for my bed! (Wag, wag, wiggle, roll on the blanket.)

"You like it don't you?"

"I do! I love it! Thank you, thank you!"

"It even matches the room."

"It's great! I can't see colors, so it could be purple and brown and it wouldn't matter."

"Now you don't have to sleep with us in the bed anymore."

"I love your bed, but I'll sleep here if you want me to."

So whereas our marriage of twenty-five years has resulted in at least 9,125 aggravating tête-à-têtes with my husband (one a day), I've yet to have one strained conversation with my dog. The dog is patient and kind and doesn't snarl because I've stored the soy sauce in the cabinet under the oven rather than in the cupboard over the microwave. The dog just hopes my husband will find the condiment, so the slab of meat he's grilling will have better flavor when I slip him a glorious scrap or two.

My dog balances our household. He exhibits the optimism that equilibrates my husband's sometimes off-putting view of the world. Don't misunderstand me. I love my husband, but I absolutely adore my furry cherub.

My husband is yelling for me from the kitchen. Seems he just kicked the dog's water bowl and is looking for the roll of paper towels to sop up the spill. I don't have the heart to tell him I just used the last one wiping the puppy's muddy paws.

Yes, the canine line is always going to be longer than the husband line at the pearly gates. Isn't it nice to know who the majority of our guardian angels will be?

Chapter 5

Panic:

A sudden, overpowering terror

We have a utopian purpose whenever we take a new dog into our families. We like to think that bringing home that adorable addition will result in hours of endless joy for both parties. We believe adopting that precious stray from the shelter will save her from certain death and us from hours of loneliness. We hope that by opening our homes to the adorable but forlorn rescue, a bad situation will turn into a happily-ever-after scene.

In most cases, our wishes do come true. We end up with well-adjusted, respectful relationships with our dogs. It takes time, but we get there. We just didn't know about the bumps along the way.

Sometimes the bumps are small—the accidents in the house, the gnawed furniture leg, the 3:00 a.m. howling, the six-foot hole in the squash garden. But when the bumps become traumatic, we often become panicked. And with good reason. Our dogs are our children, so safety becomes an overarching theme in our homes.

Panicked puppy people do strange things. They become animated under stress. They

become terrified monsters who will stop at nothing to ensure the safety of their beloved dogs. And they have no self-consciousness; those who are shy grow canine teeth, those who are slight in size morph into hulklike proportions, those who thought they didn't care that much become driving advocates for their babies.

The narratives that follow express all too well what moves us to panic mode. In "Where, Oh, Where Has My Little Dog Gone?" the temporary loss of a dog takes one woman on an unthinkable escapade. Fighting among dog siblings forces one guardian to brave the brawl in "Southpaw's in the Ring." And the natural instincts of a mother with her runt puppy push two ladies to near panic in "The Luckiest Runt."

Panicking over our dogs reaffirms what we knew but maybe weren't willing to admit: we'd do just about anything to keep them out of harm's way. There isn't a better crusade.

Where, Oh, Where Has My Little Dog Gone?

It's like a movie in slow motion. The camera pans in on a woman who is spinning in circles, going berserk, calling frantically, whistling, crying. It's pure panic, an emotional scene but one that has been played out time and time again in every household—where there's a dog.

It doesn't matter how many times it's happened. When the dog is missing, everything stops until he's found. The conversation with the husband generally goes something like this:

"Honey, have you seen the dog?"

"Nope," he says nonchalantly, never breaking his eyes from the newspaper he is reading. "Why, was I supposed to have seen the dog?"

"I can't find him."

"I wasn't looking for him."

"You don't have to be looking for him. He should just *be* here—at my feet, the way he always is."

"Maybe your feet smell."

"Sweetheart! The dog is missing."

"I'll alert the media."

That discussion is going nowhere, so rather than waste time, I move on. My chest is constricting by the second; my heart is pounding. My dog is MIA. I give up on the husband and head for the children.

I bust into my son's room, where the fifteen-year-old is glued to his computer, playing an interactive video game. He's so engrossed he doesn't even know I've entered the dungeon. I look under the piles of dirty clothes strewn across the floor.

"Have you seen the dog?" I ask, hoping my voice will carry over the rapid clicking of the keyboard and mouse.

"What dog?"

I stop, surprised he answers. "The one you asked for? The one you said you'd feed? The one you named?"

"No."

What matters is he's HOME. He's safe. He's right here, right now.

I bravely bend over and lift the skirt of his bed, hoping to see those beady little eyes staring back at me. I see only balled-up homework, gum wrappers, and a few tattered Yu-Gi-Oh trading cards.

"You mean you haven't seen the dog?"

"No. Should I have?"

I step over a pile of schoolbooks and head for the next bedroom. The scene is the same—the sixteen-year-old is also clicking away at the keyboard, trying to blow up the universe.

"Have you seen the dog?" I open his closet door. No dog in there. No answer from the kid.

"I said have you seen the dog?"

He looks up, only just realizing that I've entered the no-parent zone. He has his headphones on—video stereophonics at its

best. The volume on his computer is so loud that I can hear the commotion through the headset. He's still staring blankly at me.

"The dog!" I yell and spell it out with sign language.

"What about the dog?" he blares, not realizing he's talking louder than his video game music.

"Never mind." I leave his world and rush to the master bedroom, a room with many hiding places.

I call out the dog's name, I guess expecting a return bark—no answer. I look in the walk-in closet—no dog. I check the bathroom, the shower, the tub (yes, the tub!)—no dog. I look behind doors, under tables, between couches. No dog anywhere.

Then the gigantic fear hits. What if he went outside in the backyard and got loose? What if he dug under the gate, singing "Free at Last!" and made a fifty-yard dash for the street? What if he (gasp!) were running with a pack, sniffing garbage, and sowing his wild oats?

Out the door I rush, screaming his name until I'm hoarse. I walk the entire backyard, inspecting the fence for prisoner breaks. I see nothing. I can only do next what I'd hoped I wouldn't have to do—I'm off on a door-to-door puppy patrol.

On the first knock, I bruise my knuckles. "Hello, have you seen my dog?"

"Didn't know you owned one."

"Well, yes, he doesn't get out much, until today."

"What does it look like?"

"*He's* fawn and white and, well, chubby."

"Mmmmm. Sounds like my dog. Oliver, come. Come, Oliver!" Out trots a fat mutt with overgrown toenails and a knotted coat. A pungent odor fills the foyer, and I take a few steps backward. My dog doesn't look like that and he has never, I repeat, never stunk.

"No, my dog doesn't—"

"Haven't seen it."

"*Him*. Thanks." I rush down the steps and move to the next house.

And so I ring doorbell after doorbell, keeping my fingers crossed and holding my breath, hoping, wishing that I'll find my beloved. It's not until I turn for the house that I realize I'm in my pajamas, I've got flip-flops on, and my hair never saw a brush this morning. I'm a wreck.

When I finally give up on cold-calling, I am beat. I've never suffered like this in my life.

I feel like a funeral is in order, but then I remember I've got one last place to check: the pound.

I make the call with trembling hands and a shaky voice. "I'm looking for a lost dog," I say.

"We've got plenty here. Would you like to speak with an adoption agent?"

"No, no. *I'm* looking for my lost dog."

"You'd have to come down to the shelter. We've got entirely too many dogs to take information over the phone."

"Oh."

"But, 99 percent of the folks who've lost dogs find them the same day."

"Really?" My hopes rise.

"Yeah. Don't give up. Give it one more round. Your dog will show up."

"Thanks." I hang up, determined to find my dearly departed.

I collapse into the stuffed loveseat and begin to weep. I've lost possibly the best friend I've ever had, and I can't do anything about it. I resign that, first thing in the morning, I'll start printing flyers to post around the neighborhood. I'll call the paper and take out an ad. I'll never stop looking. No matter what.

"Oh, puppy!" I say to the room through my sobs. "Come back!"

As if he hears me and feels my pain, up he jumps from nowhere into my lap. My precious! "Where have you been?" I ask. "You scared Mama!"

Between licks and tail wags I call for my family. "The dog's home!" I announce. "I found him!"

They all come rushing into the room, wondering what the hullabaloo is about. My husband's hand is still attached to the newspaper. My oldest son has headphones over his ears. The long unattached cord is wrapped around his ankles. My youngest son is glaring at me like I need a frontal lobotomy.

"Look! I found him. I found him. He's back." I'm rubbing his fur and patting his rear like it's the first time I've ever felt a dog.

They look at each other, shake their heads, and turn to retreat, my husband back to his paper, my sons back to Computerland. They simply don't understand.

I never figured out where my dog had been. But that doesn't matter. What matters is he's home. He's safe. He's right here, right now, at my feet, right where I like him.

Southpaw's in the Ring

by Rebecca Englert

When two dogs challenge each other, the experience is both terrifying and enlightening. Natural dog confrontations are different from human-driven events, where irresponsible people make money off of Pit Bulls mangling each other in an arena. True dog face-offs might be for dominance or possession or even humping rights. These battles can take place right inside your house with no cajoling from the guardians. It's dog-eat-dog, and it's expensive, frustrating, and downright scary.

Male dogs will fight for a female in heat or for dominance. They will fight until one dog is whipped. The underdog always knows when it's time to throw in the towel. The top dog will usually release the other just to allow him to feel ashamed and beaten down. This keeps the loser in submission to the dominant dog. It is all psychological with males.

I can't put them in time-out forever, restriction DOESN'T work, and counseling is not an option.

Although some may think male dogs would be the more aggressive fighters, the female is truly the "bitch." Female dogs want to kill. Come on, ladies! You know how that female aggression plays out. She-dogs will fight to the death almost every time. Even when a female dog is obviously runner up, she will continue the fight until the other dog kills her. A mere dirty look or sarcastic bark—that is all that is necessary to set a pair of females off. Ah, the mystery of the weaker sex! Well, maybe females aren't the frail ones, in this case.

As any dog owner knows, dogs are very social animals. They need to be a part of a group. If there is only one dog in a house, then the lone dog forms a pack with his people. Multiple dogs in a household form their own pack, similar to their wolf ancestors in the wild. Every pack has an alpha male and an alpha female. Of course, if all the dogs are the same sex, that just

breaks down to *the* alpha dog. This dog is in charge of all the others and everything they do. The alpha will control them all and will be sure to let them know their place. Alphas demand first rights to food, ultimate respect, and every raw hide that they take a fancy to. Woe to any dog that potties then kicks up the dirt in this dog's yard.

What happens when you have more than one dog trying to be the alpha? Dog fight! To the death, I might add. And having only female dogs, I have seen my share of fights.

I have three beautiful girls. Dixie is a Jack (Parson) Russell Terrier mixed with a Bull Terrier. She's the little one. She's happy-go-lucky and could care less who rules the house. Sable is a Rottweiler–German Shepherd Dog mix (Dominant? Absolutely!) Piper is a Foxhound mixed with who-knows-what. Sable and Piper together weigh over one hundred pounds, and, of course, they are the two that can't agree on who the boss is going to be.

Sable has led the competition with three very bloody victories, but Piper refuses to accept defeat. Despite stitches, staples, bandages, painkillers, and antibiotics, Piper feels the battle must go on until she wins the title. (Never mind the $500 a month that it costs me to be a VIP at the after-hours emergency clinic!)

When these brawls occur, luck has it that I'm at home by myself. My husband has yet to deal with the fury. I alone try to break apart two dogs that almost equal my body weight. These melees always happen when I am not in the room, so I don't get a chance to stop them when the girls are still in the posturing stage. By the time I hear them, they are in a frenzy, and nothing in this world will break them apart.

Other people are loaded with advice when your dogs are locked in battle. "Pour water on them," they recommend. Sure. That's like giving Tyson a between-round squirt from his water bottle—quite a refreshing treat. My gals just busy themselves with ripping off hunks of shoulder. "Yell in their ears," they suggest. Okeydoke. So what am I supposed to do with two deaf dogs that are STILL FIGHTING? "Pull their tails," they propose. Just what I want to be doing when these enraged dogs let go of each other and turn on me. I mean, hey, I didn't want to live past today anyway. When dogs get wound up from fighting, nothing, including your hand, is off-limits. They have crossed over to the dark side.

Probably the worst part of my situation is the confusion on how to stop the rage. When your dog is being attacked, you usually focus on the dog that is attacking your dog. But when they are *both* your dogs, which one do you chastise? You are willing to hurt someone else's dog when it is hurting yours, but when you own them both, which one gets the short end of the stick? Which one gets kicked, punched, or mace-sprayed? How can you do that to one you love?

There is little repercussion for the fighters. I can't put them in time-out forever, restriction doesn't work, and counseling is not an option. I can't work them around the house as punishment or make them apologize to each other. The best I can do is keep refereeing, and I am turning pro at that. In fact, if my credit card holds out long enough, I may just write a book on how to overcome dog fights. I could title it *Ten Ways to Guarantee Being Bitten While Trying to Break Up Fighting Dogs*. I could do some book signings, and maybe a talk show or two. Who knows, perhaps the after-hours emergency vet I keep in business will let me advertise my book in his office.

Now, if we could just get these confounded dogs to behave!

———

The Luckiest Runt

When Brandy, my purebred American Pit Bull Terrier, became pregnant, my roommate and I moved her from her backyard doghouse to the cooler screened porch to escape the summer doldrums. A dog of habit, she'd sneak away to her doghouse, and we'd find her half in, half out—her large stomach inside the shady doghouse, her head peering out hoping for a cool breeze. Brandy very much resembled Winnie the Pooh stuck in the rabbit hole.

Soon though, temperatures rose and Brandy dug a deep hole beneath the doghouse, which enabled her to inch backward into the opening. There, her round tummy met cold, dark earth. As much as we encouraged her to remain on the porch, she spent the rest of her pregnancy in her personal dugout.

We tried everything to keep Brandy on the breezy tiled patio. We bought fancy beds and blankets, laced the floor with a host of toys and treats, and kept a fresh supply of food and water for her. She'd give an obligatory sniff around the padded coverlet and an occasional chew on a squeaky toy, but for the most part our efforts were for naught.

Before she went into labor, she paced from the porch to the doghouse and back, her big belly tipping the edge of the wide grass blades. She wanted to deliver those puppies in her own territory, but she was respectful of our wishes. She consented to giving birth on the porch but clearly let us know that when the hype was over, she was moving back out to her backyard bungalow.

The pups came on a full-mooned midnight, four tiny female beauts mottled with brown, black, and white; and one miniscule male runt, solid black. Downy soft and fragile, they were

Downy soft and fragile, they were quite possibly the most WONDERFUL puppies I'd ever laid eyes on.

quite possibly the most wonderful puppies I'd ever laid eyes on.

The little one in particular melted my heart. He fit in the palm of my hand like a chocolate cupcake, and his tiny paws were no bigger than thumbtacks. He was the first one out and got tossed to the side quickly while Brandy concentrated on birthing the others. I knew if he survived, he'd be lucky, so that's what I named him.

Brandy settled into motherhood, staying on the porch with her newborns, nursing them, cleaning them, loving them. As the weeks went on, Lucky always seemed to be getting pushed aside to let the fatter, rounder, stronger sisters get to the milk. He hadn't gained much weight, and I was afraid he wasn't going to make it. Somehow, though, he hung on, as if he wanted to live up to his name.

Summer rains came early, locking the new canine family onto the porch. This pleased us—we could slip through the sliding glass doors and play with the babies without tromping through the wet yard. I'd take turns petting each pup, noting where each liked to be rubbed, making alliances, etching out each one's personality. By now the girls were over double the size of Lucky. He still resembled a black baby bat. Perhaps his miniature size was why I'd give him special attention. Scooping him up, I'd tickle him under his chin, and he'd look at me with tiny black eyes no bigger than BBs.

"I love you," I'd tell him, and he'd lick the tip of my pinky finger in reply.

But three weeks after the puppies arrived, I received a frantic call at work from my roommate.

"One of the pups is missing!" she screamed at the other end of the receiver.

"What do you mean?" I blurted. "Have you looked under the porch furniture?"

"I've looked everywhere! He's just gone!" I didn't have to ask which one—I already knew by the use of the pronoun. Lucky was the only boy in the litter.

"I'm on my way."

I raced home through a terrible gray storm, putting my life in jeopardy as I exceeded the speed limit and flew through a line of yellow caution lights. The car screeched into the driveway, and I flew through the house to the back porch, where I began repeating the search that my roommate had performed earlier. After ransacking the area, Lucky was still nowhere to be found.

"Maybe he's in the back garden," I wailed, trying to hold back the tears. I pushed open the screen door and began a search of the yard. The rain was bucketing down on my body, but I wasn't concerned with getting drenched. If I didn't find Lucky, I'd remain wet for weeks from weeping.

"Step lightly!" my roommate cautioned. "He's so small; he can't even clear the grass."

"Lucky!" I called the name that he did not yet know belonged to him. "Lucky, where are you?"

Brandy was on our heels, running around us in circles, becoming alarmed by our cries for her runt. We almost tripped over the mother several times.

"Brandy, get back to the porch!" I commanded.

She dropped her rear to the wet ground and gave a rebuttal bark.

"Go!" I pointed to the patio. "Back inside!"

Brandy remained still.

"Wait!" my roommate blurted. "Lucky's the runt."

"Duh," I replied. "Why do you think it's critical that we find him?"

"Mothers sometimes move their runts away from the others."

"Well, that's stupid!" I snapped.

"I bet she knows where Lucky is. Let's ask her."

My roommate knelt down and stroked Brandy's rain soaked head. In a calm low voice, she asked, "Where's your little boy, Brandy? Find him. Go find Lucky."

Just as she'd done a thousand times before, Brandy bolted for the doghouse and plopped down inside.

"All she wants is to get out of the rain," I complained. "She's no help."

"Not necessarily," my roommate disagreed. "Let's check the dugout."

We ran to the old wooden doghouse and pulled Brandy out by her collar. I squatted on all fours, my hands and knees sinking into the mushy sod, and stuck my head and shoulders into the doghouse. "No Lucky."

Backing out, I placed my hands on top of the shelter and gave a firm push to shove myself up out of the muck. The wooden house dropped a few feet and a wave of muddy water splashed over our feet.

My friend and I snapped our heads toward each other, and the looks on our faces were identical.

"Lucky!" we bellowed in unison.

With all our might we pushed the doghouse onto its rear wall until it balanced against the wooden fence. Floating at the top of the brown slush was the littlest angel, looking like a swollen lima bean—our Lucky.

I scooped him up and started rubbing him with my shirt, trying to remove the bits of mud that were wedged in his nostril slits. I turned my head sideways, drew him to my face, and placed my ear on his small chest, trying to listen for a heartbeat, any sign that said he was alive.

The rain had picked up and began to beat down on our backs as we stood huddled over Lucky and prayed him on, stroked his little body, moved his listless legs up and down, trying to get some circulation.

Without hesitation, I opened my mouth and placed it over his nose and mouth. With short spurts of breath, I administered a sort of puppy CPR, not really knowing if this was something that would work, but being careful not to breathe out too much air lest his minute lungs explode.

Suddenly, I felt a wiggle in my hands, like a fish on a hook. Lucky was alive!

"Come on, little guy!" I encouraged. "Breathe!"

Lucky wriggled again, and his eyes flew open. They were on me, asking me what took so long, thanking me for believing in him, begging me to take him to his mother and his sisters.

"There's my Lucky!" I announced with satisfaction. As I stared lovingly into the face of that little runt, I realized that life really was like a roll of the dice. One minute Lucky's number was up; the next minute he was safe. One thing was sure, though: nothing could stop him now.

Chapter 6

Ingenuity:
Inventive skill or imagination; cleverness

We humans like to think of ourselves as ingenious. We always have the answer, and we can find it if we don't. We are cognitively superior to any animal on the planet—until we meet up with our dogs, who, with no pompousness at all, give us a new perspective regarding their keen abilities. Rather than scoff at the competition, however, we puff out our chests. We taunt society with "My dog is smarter than yours" bumper stickers, and we take every opportunity to tell stories about their jaw-dropping skills. We never tire of boasting about how clever our dogs are.

This entirely true chapter titled *Ingenuity* celebrates the wonderful talents our dogs possess and demonstrates how we, in turn, react to those talents. In "Spellbound," the parents of a pair of Border Collies resort to extreme measures to outwit their two spelling bee champs. "All in a Day's Work" spotlights Ajax the Amazing as he outwits a gymnasium maze. Finally, "Tug-of-Peace" brings to light the incredible rescue story of two Texas dogs, Sophie and Little Bean.

Our dogs have something we humans usually don't have. Not only are they cute *and* well-behaved, they're smart, too. You rarely find that combination in people. But you do find it with dogs. Now, go put that bumper sticker on your car.

Paws and Smell the World

Spellbound

by Laura Kangas

As a responsible dog parent, you expect to do many things throughout the life span of your pets. You expect to teach them to be obedient, train them to go outside to answer nature's call, instruct them not to beg for food, and encourage them to be good canine citizens in general. You coach them all you can and hope that one day some of it will actually "stick" and that they will remember the things you worked hard to teach them. But what happens if your canine companions actually learn something you did *not* teach them; something they mastered on their own? What if they learned to s-p-e-l-l?

As most Border Collie companions will tell you, this particular breed is extremely intelligent. The Border Collie aptitude, however, is not just limited to the customary dog duties. We have all seen numerous Border Collies acting in movies or commercials

We could no longer utter the words that sent them into an EXPLOSION of flying fur and dripping slobber.

and participating in various demanding canine sports. As the parents of two Border Collies for the past eight years, my husband and I have learned to be creative in ways we never before considered. We have no (human) children, and many of these daily adjustments would be expected if we had preschool kids, not dogs.

It all *really* started a few years ago when we lived in North Carolina. We were fortunate enough to live next to a neighborhood park and took full advantage of having three-plus acres at our disposal. On a daily basis, we walked to the park to play Frisbee. We began to notice that we could not utter *any* of these words, in *any* context, without the dogs becoming extremely excited. The mere mention of the word *play* or *Frisbee* was enough to initiate the thrashing of tails against walls, heavy breathing, bouncing and jumping, and, in extreme cases, frantic barking.

Of course, we thought we were smarter than they were, so we started to spell the words. We assumed we could circumvent this whole fanatical display of "dogg-ie-motion" by simply spelling the trigger words that sent our dogs into such a frenzy.

So in our house, matrimonial communication became tedious and methodical: "I'm going to take the d-o-g-s to the p-a-r-k."

"N-o-w?"

"Y-e-s."

This exercise in futility lasted only a few weeks, until *they knew*. They listened with intensity and watched our lips form the letters, and their eyes and hearts told us that *they simply knew.*

Many people argue that dogs cannot spell. Our friends are skeptics who insist that dogs only learn a certain pattern of speech or tone of voice and certainly are not spelling. We disagree. We know the prowess of the Border Collie. While many other breeds are certainly capable of this same phonetic gift, Border Collies excel at it and, if I might add, thoroughly delight in it.

Many times we put our theory to the test:

Wife to dogs: "Where's the f-r-u-i-t?"

Dogs: No interest

Wife to dogs: "Where's the f-r-o-g?"

Dogs: Nothing

Wife to dogs: "Where's the F-r-i-s-b-e-e?"

Dogs: Standing at full attention, ears up, tails out, heads turning, looking for IT!

Case closed.

And so it continued. We could no longer utter the words that sent them into an explosion of flying fur and dripping slobber. The next hurdle was inventing new words and phrases for things that had once been commonplace. The easiest decision was to no longer use the word p-a-r-k. Since most parks have a name, such as Fishweir Park or Memorial Park, we became proper noun park—specific.

Husband to wife: "I'm going to Fishweir with the dogs."

The decision to use the park name provided immediate relief for this particular stressful situation. However, there was still *the word* F-r-i-s-b-e-e. We experimented with using only hand gestures as a substitute for *the word*, but finally settled on *disk object.*

Husband to wife: "I'm taking the dogs to Fishweir to do disc object."

This new approach has now become our standard way of speaking, and we find ourselves uttering this new language even when the dogs are not present.

Husband to wife at restaurant: "When we get home, I'm going to take the dogs to Fishweir to do the disk object."

Other words such as *place* and *thing* have also assumed a more prominent role in our daily vocabulary, even when there are no dogs listening.

Wife to husband: "When we get home from the grocery store, let's take the dogs to the place to do the thing." This makes perfect sense. Husband agrees.

A small sampling of words that seem to have been banished forever (or at least for the next eight to ten years) from our vocabulary are: p-a-r-k, p-l-a-y, r-i-d-e, t-o-y, t-r-e-a-t, b-a-l-l, and, of course, F-r-i-s-b-e-e.

Fast-forward ten years. I cannot help but wonder if once our Border Collies pass over the Rainbow Bridge we will continue with this bizarre way of communicating in our cryptic, customized dog lingo. What once took a great deal of effort is now routine and involuntary, much like breathing or blinking. Will we continue to use it out of mere habit or to pay homage to them after their passing?

P-r-o-b-a-b-l-y s-o.

All in a Day's Work

Ajax was a gym hound. He grew up in the gym, lived in the gym, worked in the gym, played in the gym. He was the most socialized dog I'd ever seen, meeting and greeting at least four to five hundred different people a week—female gymnasts of every age, shape, and size; proud parents who took their spectator seats in the bleachers; and coaches and judges from all over the nation who'd take part in occasional gymnastics meets. Ajax was an icon; an all-American gymnastics mascot; a dog who modeled the strength, tenacity, and go-get-'em-ness that his owner hoped the young gymnasts would adopt.

The sixty pound white bulldog got picked on a lot, but he never seemed to care. The fact that he was invited to and attended every statewide and national gymnastics meet (no-dogs-allowed hotels included) told

He'd shuffle across the floor mat with that fat-bottomed gait and petulant smile.

him he was loved. He'd shuffle across the floor mat with that fat-bottomed gait and petulant smile and go about his business as if he had as much right to show off his floor routine as any other gymnast did. For good luck, the girls would pat his rear with their white chalk-covered palms before they conquered their uneven bars routine. Folks called to him with words other than his given name, and he learned to respond (or not) to them. Pig, Pizza the Hut, The Best, Sweetest Man—no matter. Ajax was in charge, and he knew it.

The extent of Ajax's intelligence outweighed the strength in his jaws (he was capable of picking up a fifty-pound bowling ball and traipsing over to the balance beam). Part of the after-hours entertainment for the coaching staff was to challenge Ajax with yet another puzzle, and—with all bets on—the group would kick back with drinks and snacks and watch the dog think his way through mazes with which even a human would have trouble.

The ladder was often arranged in the center of the gym floor with a red balloon tied to the top. Like Eeyore, Ajax had an affinity for balloons; therefore, the balloon was motivational for the dog. The vertical steep was, of course, canine-impossible, so a mix of foam blocks was thrown haphazardly around the setup as teasers. Like a challenger from *Survivor*, Ajax pushed the blocks to and from the ladder, stacked them on top of each other, and jumped up closer and closer until he finally reached his goal. The mastery involved the challenge of how to arrange the blocks for the closest and safest route. The dog was a mastermind.

One of the greatest challenges Ajax ever conquered was the feat called Fast Mouth. A simple blue racquetball, thrown with a windup pitch at no less than sixty miles per hour, resulted in a catch by Ajax that was comparable to Mr. Miyagi from *The Karate Kid* catching a fly with a pair of chopsticks.

Day after day, Ajax never ceased to amaze his fans. Just when they thought he couldn't crack a humanly designed code, Ajax and his determination would prove the crew wrong. He was the old dog with new tricks. His owner was as proud of his accomplishments as he was of those of any of his top-performing gymnasts. The gym became known as much for the dog as it was for the internationally ranked athletes.

When it was time for Ajax to retire, he did so quietly. He went outside to his favorite morning spot and simply breathed his last breath. The "pig in the sunshine," as his owner used to call him, remains a legacy to this day. There's never been another Ajax in the gym, and there never will be.

No one really knows if the dog learned his skill and agility from the gymnasts or if it was the other way around. One thing's for sure, though: for a sixty-pound pig, he was the most intelligent, persistent, and determined pooch in the sport.

Tug-of-Peace

LB and Sophie weren't always the best of friends. In fact, they didn't care for each other at all. Call it women's war. Two strong females, they learned that being friends gave them more strength than being at odds. It's the classic saga—two girls, jealous and embittered, find themselves thrown together in a life-changing situation and become part of a sisterhood of sorts. The difference here is that LB and Sophie are both my dogs.

LB—which is short for Little Bean—is a Beagle/Dachshund mix who lived down the street and was perpetually abused: hit with a shovel, beaten until wounded (and secretly nursed by me). I'd swab her with medicine and send her back home, fingers crossed, hoping for the best. Little Bean would return the next day, the medicine wiped off, the cuts exposed. Finally, I resorted to stapling notes on her collar saying, "Don't wipe off the medicine!"

She broke the mold by saving a life, and that's where this tale takes its spin, 'cause the life that she saved was Little Bean's soul. Soph was a DOG'S BEST FRIEND.

Despite her skinny, mangled self, I thought she was cute, even after bearing a litter of pups that made her look even scrawnier.

Not able to stand the daily beatings, I swore that as soon as LB's puppies were independent, I'd steal her away from her owners. And that's exactly what I did. I dog-napped that three-year-old canine. That was the best and only crime I've ever committed.

Little Bean has grown into a barking brat who thinks she's a Great Dane. She loves my attention, and I love giving it to her. At night when the family is asleep, she slithers off the curved sectional of the couch and slips into my daughter's bed. Shortly before we rise, she slinks back to the sofa. When we shuffle into the room, she lifts her groggy head as if to say, "I've been here all night." I know her tricks, but I don't want to spoil her fun.

Sophie, who is our Blue Heeler mix, was a six-week-old giveaway,

dragged home from the Liberty County Fair Petting Zoo, where our son went on a field trip. He fell in love with her. So did I. A possessive puppy—one who never wanted to share her tennis balls—Sophie spent a lot of hours in time-out over her toys. She wasn't much for sharing me, either. Beanie's barks for my attention made Sophie furious. She wanted everything for her own.

Pairing the girls was like putting two beauty queens in a room. Both would fight for the top spot, and I was forever pulling them apart and stowing all the toys away in a box.

That, though, has since changed due to an event that is both unbelievable and affirming. Unbelievable because I'd never in a million years think that a dog could be so persistent; affirming because I know just how brave, loving, and clever Sophie really is. My two dogs are not man's (or woman's) best friend; they are each other's best friend. And it happened through a very bizarre accident that was followed by a very intelligent rescue.

On that hot Texas morning, I heard a loud ruckus out back near the ditch behind our house. The neighborhood dogs were barking like mad, and at first I did not give them much attention. But as I picked out the individual dog voices, I realized I did not hear Sophie or Beanie. I hurried outside following the noise, and on my way out to the back yard, I detected Little Bean yelping in distress—a muffled whine.

I ran to the noise and saw Sophie with Bean's back leg in her mouth. I yelled at Sophie to let go of Beanie. Why in the world was she clamped to Little Bean's leg? This latest fight was the last straw. I marched toward the dogs, determined to discipline these two troublemakers once and for all.

I had almost reached the doggy duo, when I halted. A huge alligator had Little Bean's head clamped in its jaws. On instinct, I ran to our backyard fire pit and grabbed a concrete pipe. Dragging it down the hill, I threw it beside the gator's wide head. Its jaws opened wide in reaction to the splash, and it angrily hissed my way. In that split second, Sophie dragged Bean up the hill and into the yard, not letting go until she reached the back door. Bean turned and gave a perfunctory bark at Sophie. When I looked back, the gator was gone. All that remained were the dig marks in the mud showing how deep Sophie had braced herself. That dog was in it for the long haul and was not going to let go until Little Bean went with her. I'm convinced it was a combination of Sophie's aggravating sense of possession and her acute intelligence that saved Little Bean's life.

Today, LB follows Sophie everywhere, and that makes me feel better, given that we are still waiting on permission from the game warden to have that gator removed. The girls bark together, roll around together, and tear things up together. I know in my heart that if Sophie were in dire straits, LB would come to her rescue swiftly and purposefully, just as Sophie did for her. After all, sisterhood is a serious notion, and when there's an opportunity to play tug-of-peace with your sister, well, that's exactly what you do.

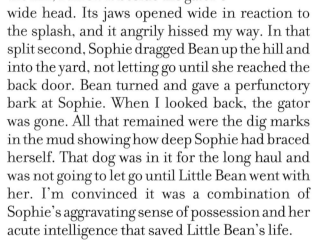

Chapter 7

Hope:

To wish for something with expectation of its fulfillment

Do you remember the first time you wished for a dog? The stories you heard about the sweet relationships between man and his best friend curled the edges of your heart and made you want to experience the joy for yourself. And once you held your pup for the first time, the hopes for a beautiful relationship grew, sealing the positive opportunities forever.

The feeling of hope is reciprocal. Imagine how many times a dog wishes for a person! This poignant chapter entitled *Hope* explores the expectations and dreams not only of dog owners but also of dogs themselves, and it solidifies how important humans and dogs are to each other's existence.

In "Five Days Stray," a traveler contemplates the fate of a canine drifter and comes to a life-changing decision for both parties. A dog is lost at sea, but his unlikely survival propels him to national fame as a symbol of hope in "Coconut Harry." And "The Nine Lives of Mac," a tale of determination, proves that some folks and dogs need each other whether they think they do or not.

Often sparking the melancholy in us, those unfortunate journeys some dogs take offer us hope for peace and love and togetherness. Therefore, hope can never be dismissed as an insignificant virtue. It provides us with goals that are worth seeking and satisfying. And when the goals include our dogs, our lives are thoroughly enriched.

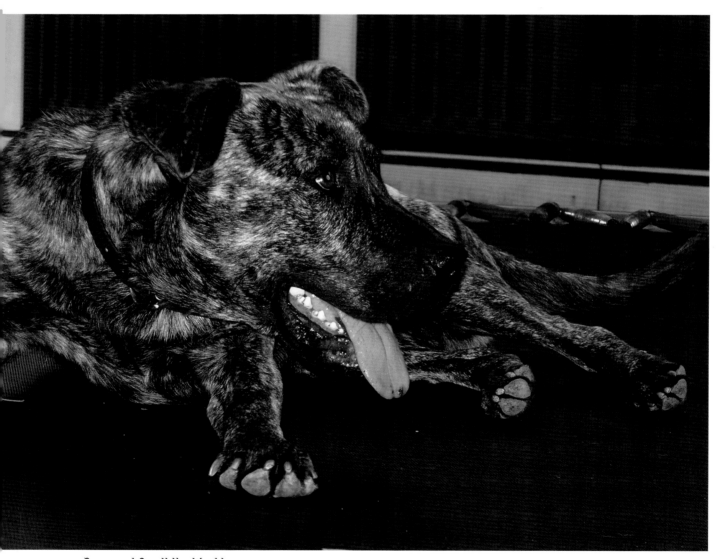

Paws and Smell the World

Five Days Stray

by Rebecca Englert

I see him for the first time in the middle of the morning, sniffing a tall gray garbage can. He is too weak to even jump up onto the metal can's side for a better smell. He stands numb, and he reminds me of a city bum looking for a scrap meal.

He turns to gaze at me as I drive by. His sad eyes say that he has known hurt. They tell me that he is hungry. They ask, "Why won't anyone help me? Where are my humans?"

I drive on and think, "It must have been a horrible person who threw a dog out in the woods like that to starve to death or freeze or get splattered by an automobile."

I don't stop. I just keep driving.

The next day I see him trotting down the road with a frantic gait, a fast and scattered run. His whole being—the way he carries himself—screams that he is desperate. He rushes toward every car that zooms past, but he is

He gives me a sweet kiss on the wrist. A seal to a wonderful DEAL.

quickly pushed back by the furious dust from the road.

Is he searching for the one who dropped him off? Could he really be hoping that they were going to come back for him? Do dogs really think that way?

I don't even press my brakes. I've got to get to work.

Day three, and there he is again. Ragged and sad, longing for a whistle, a pat on the back, someone to take an interest.

I ask myself how long this dog will have to wander around before somebody does something. Won't anyone feed him or take him in? What is wrong with people in this world? How can they see a dog starving and neglected like this, day after day, and not help?

I think to myself as I drive by, "People are so cruel."

On the fourth day, he is there—old faithful, sitting slumped by the road. He is so skinny that

I cannot believe he is still able to walk. His ribs look like a washing board. He is so broken now that he does not even look at the cars as they whiz by. He merely exists.

I am upset. All these surrounding houses and nobody will help him. How can people leave this dog to die by the roadside? So many folks racing by—and nobody will do anything.

As I ride on I think, "Our society is hopeless."

It is yet another day, and he is there again, as reliable as the traffic on this road, as constant as my daily journey to the job. Once more, I fume about the indifference of people. I roll forward, peering into my rear view mirror, until he is but a brown speck.

But wait. How could I have missed this before? I am a person too! As Gandhi said, "You must be the change you wish to see in the world." I wheel my car around, pull up beside him, and stare at his matted fur. His eyes meet mine, and I see that I have been five-days mistaken. He still *does* have a little hope left in him. I can see it in his soul as I step out of the car. I can tell by his weak attempt to wag his tail as I reach out to pat his head. He gives me a sweet kiss on the wrist. A seal to a wonderful deal.

We're both on a new path as we drive home together.

I have given him his trust back, and he has given me the realization that sorrow can be healed one courageous step at a time.

Coconut Harry

by Mark Smith

He had his head out the back window as he left Key Largo on U.S. 1. Salt air. A scent unfamiliar, but not unwelcome. Different from the continental air he'd been born into in Oklahoma two years earlier. But this new scent came from water that would define his life, rewrite his name. Harry didn't know any of that at the moment—didn't know that he'd be a golden example of courage and hope to thousands of people, and wouldn't have cared anyway. What mattered was the woman in the front seat, his owner, close enough for him to lean forward and lick the back of her ear as she drove her Golden Re-triever and herself to-ward their new home in Florida's Lower Keys. She drove Harry toward his status—though still years away—as a legend.

Other people called his owner Naomi, and he saw her respond when they said that name. She had chosen a

His message to them was always the same:
HOPE FLOATS——like a coconut.

house near water, and something deep within him was drawn to water in a way he couldn't resist, and he didn't. Down the sloping yard he'd run and take flying leaps into the canal, just past the dock, past the large boat that took them for rides on the ocean. He swam every day until the swim alone failed to satisfy.

Ever curious, he ignored his ball one morning and walked instead to the hard lumpy things that fell from the palm trees. Barely able to hold one in his mouth, he bit into it nevertheless, chewed, carried it to the water, and dropped it in as he stared at his reflection. The new toy floated, and he wanted it, jumped in after it, and brought it ashore. Finding the whole exercise amusing, he discovered a new diversion. A new passion. Soon, and from then on, when Naomi's friends came to visit, they added a word to his name. "Coconut Harry," they'd call, and he'd come with a damp lumpy thing in his mouth and drop it at their feet because this always, always seemed to make them happy enough to kneel and pet him.

Coconuts fell. The wind blew. Every day was warm outside, but the cool tile of Naomi's house was a place for Harry to relax. Naomi sewed clothes for him, which he never minded wearing because she took him to places where lots of other pets, too, were dressed in something other than their own coats. But to him, many pets seemed uncomfortable, especially after they all stood in a line with Coconut Harry in the room where people ate, drank, and smoked and always clapped when Harry's name was called. He liked the people, and they liked him.

This was Harry's life. These were Harry's friends. And so it went, from one hurricane season to the next. "You're nine," Naomi said one day, but Harry didn't understand the words. He did understand when she said the word *ride*, though, and soon they did ride again. Not in the car but on the boat. She said other things to him: "Jump on. Stay away from the railing. You can go below decks. Sleep in the V-berth." It all sounded familiar, as familiar as the rocking of the big boat on the windy waters of the Atlantic Ocean.

Naomi came to him soon after he couldn't see land anymore. Why the place got smaller mystified him on the way out to sea, but he loved to see the trees that dropped his toys get larger when the boat went back to the dock. It was new and exciting every time. Naomi petted his head as these impressions raced through it. Then she turned and climbed the ladder he could not ascend. He tried three times long before, but his legs ached in places now, and he knew she'd come back down anyway.

Harry dozed on deck. He was awakened by new movement beneath him that pressed him against the wooden surface then bounced him off of it. He stood and shook himself, spreading his legs for balance. Curious, he went to the railing. It bounced again, and he braced against the change of his weight when it dipped and bounced once more. The boat threw him into the cool water. As he came up for air, he watched the boat disappear, with neither Naomi nor her friend in sight.

Naomi folded her navigational charts and put them by the magazine she'd been reading. Checking her watch, she realized an hour had passed since she had looked in on Harry. Leaving her friend at the helm, she descended the ladder to the deck below to find no dog there, so she went into the cabin and called. No response. There were few places to look, and she checked those frantically. Then back to the deck and a call up to the helm to turn the boat around. Harry was gone.

The Florida Keys sit like leaves on a pond, some leaves large, some small, but the pond itself is a large one: from where she stood on the yacht in the Atlantic Ocean, there was only more ocean to her east and the Gulf of Mexico to her west. She scanned the dips and troughs of the waves as far as she could see, straining for sight of a wet golden head and splashing paws. The boat retraced its course, circled, crisscrossed the path, but no dog could be seen. It just couldn't be, could it? Was Harry really lost at sea?

Marine radio calls filled the airwaves. Telephones rang. Boats of all sizes left docks around the Lower Keys. The Coast Guard joined the flotilla searching for the lost dog that had already developed a loyal band of admirers from Marathon to Key West. They searched until dusk and vowed to return again the next morning at first light. They did, too, that morning, and the next, and for days afterward. A multitude of islands and sandbars were scoured. No dog was found, and the search was called off.

Exhausted, thirsty, and confused, Harry shook the weight of the sticky salt water from his coat in a brief spasm of rallied strength, then dropped to the sand just past the waterline on shore. The day was growing light, and he could begin to see trees but not his house, no docks, and no boats. No coconuts. But he would not

have chosen to play, had no strength or desire after swimming all night. He slept where he lay until sounds of boats awakened him, but they were far away.

The day was hot and the trees farther up the shoreline offered shade. He made his way under their cover and found puddles of water that tasted like water that fell from the sky, the place where his toys came from; and in drinking it he found it didn't burn his throat the way the water in which he'd been swimming had the day before. He drank and felt better and looked up, surprised to see other animals of a type he'd never seen before. They looked like small people, and they pointed, smiled, screamed, chattered, and ran away when he moved toward them. Up into the trees they went as he continued to walk in their direction. He barked and they disappeared behind the leaves. As light and dark came and went again and again, he was never able to get close to them, but he always smelled them and heard them moving and chattering, just out of sight.

Naomi removed the damp tissue from her eyes and tapped the calendar with her finger on each of the eight days that had passed since Harry had fallen overboard. Eight days. It was hard to continue hoping, but what if he was still out there somewhere, what if he was hoping she'd find him? What was hope, she thought to herself, if not the courage to continue when logic said to give up? Harry wouldn't give up, she believed, and for as long as possible, longer than it had been so far, neither would she.

The knock at her door startled her, and she wiped her eyes again, expecting to greet a friend or even a stranger who was there to make another offer of help. When she opened the door, she opened it on a new phase of her life: "They found him. They found Harry. He's alive." She hugged and kissed the messenger, then set out for the reunion.

Eight days after falling overboard, Coconut Harry was discovered on the beach of a small island used for primate research. As a local boatman transported a researcher to the island for the weekly trip taking food and vitamins to the monkeys, they spotted another animal sitting calmly on the beach. "That looks like a dog," said the researcher. As they grew closer, the boatman exclaimed, "That's no dog! That's Coconut Harry, and he's going home to Miss Naomi."

Harry did go home—to a hero's welcome; to a television appearance on *The Late Show with David Letterman*; to acclaim in songs, in newspaper articles, and in children's school art classes; and even to become the subject of a nationally televised episode of a show about amazing stories, mysteries, and miracles. To most people, the miracle was not only that he had been found alive and well but also that nautical charts revealed that he had swum five miles to the island where he was finally rescued: that fact was a miracle full of mystery.

Harry heard the doorbell and responded with a muted "Woof." In his mouth was a toy, one of his favorites, that went everywhere with him, especially to greet another of the increasingly large band of his admirers who dropped by for a visit. The visitors always looked happy; they hugged him, they wiped

their eyes with their hands. His message to them was always the same, as he lay the mushy brown fruit of the palm tree at their feet: Hope floats. Like a coconut.

Who knows what happened out in the water while Harry was alone?

It may be a green sea turtle guided him toward home.

We all know the sea holds mystery we'll never understand.

It may have been Flipper was the skipper that steered him to dry land.

Coconut Harry stayed alive somehow.

Harry, Coconut Harry, you're a legend now.

(From the song "Coconut Harry," copyright © 1998, Mark Andrew Smith)

The Nine Lives of Mac

He wandered into our hearts on at least his fifth life. His hard-knock past was apparent by the broken, crimped tail, the asphalt hardened pads of his crooked feet, the 500 fleas that nested in his wire-bristled fur, and the fact that he smelled like sun-baked motor oil.

We named him Mac based on the first half of his breed—Scottish Terrier mixed with Dachshund. The merge made for a sore sight—he was miserably low to the ground and suffered from a large bottom scrape where his chest sagged down to the sidewalk. His front legs were knock-kneed, and his rump was oversized, and to top it off, his personality was a bit frumpy and ill-tempered. He was a hotdog in a kilt, a dog with a little man's attitude, and when he won the city's Ugliest Dog Contest, we didn't know whether to be proud or embarrassed.

My mother often hoped he would just go away in search of a sixth life in another neighborhood, but my father

Mac would race after the truck, his two-inch-long legs blurring like BRISTLES on a push broom.

was convinced he was a jewel of a dog. Mother was allergic to him, so she spent five long years sneezing. Daddy delighted in him, so he snuck the dog inside where, over time, the celery colored shag carpet became as black as Mac's fur and stunk as badly as he did.

Mac became Daddy's sidekick. Where Daddy went, Mac went. Digging through dumpsters for treasures, strolling to the nearby boat ramp, gardening in the yard—Mac did it all. They were inseparable outsiders who loved the land.

Mac was an alley dog, running the streets in the evening, visiting the back doors of the nearby restaurants. He was a bad apple, associating with the herds of stray cats that battled at midnight over pizza crust and fried catfish crumbs. Three o'clock in the morning was not sacred for this scrapper. Through the heightened hisses of feline fighting, Mac's sharp bark cut through the black night air as he'd duke it out for garbage food. One night, the cats won, and Mac—scratched, bitten, and bleeding—limped home, ready to give up his gallivanting and start his sixth life as a dumpster dog reformed.

But his itch for traveling got the better of him, and on a hot summer afternoon, we lost Mac—or more precisely, Mac lost us. Mother was elated; Daddy was devastated. His best friend was gone. Two depressing weeks went by, and Mother stopped sneezing. The calm was too much for Daddy, and he went on a ten-mile search for the dog. When Daddy rounded the corner of the street in his old Ford Falcon, there was Mac, hanging out the window as the car raced toward the house, his tongue draped long like he'd been on a journey through a dry desert.

"I'll be damned," said Mother. "He's back." Life seven began.

But Mac's lucky-numbered life didn't last long. Running would be his downfall, and that nasty habit of running finally caught up with him. He hated the mailman worse than any dog ever did, but his size was no threat to the tall, long-legged postman who laughed at the runt.

"All bark and no bite," he'd say, and hopping back into his mail truck, he'd speed off to the next house. With every ounce of go-get-him-ness, Mac would race after the truck, his two-inch-long legs blurring like bristles on a push broom, his jaws snapping at the tires like an insulted alligator. Mac spent the last moment of life seven rolling up and over the rear tire of the truck, and like Superdog, he never missed a step, but fell back onto the gravel, performed a one-and-a-half somer-sault and continued the race right slap into life number eight.

Eight was particularly hard for Mac. He was older and his hips were so worn that he couldn't scratch the fleas very well, and they got the better of him. His social nightlife diminished, and he rarely did anything but sleep or hitch a ride from Daddy, who had had a stroke and got around on an electric golf cart. The two friends did a daily tour of duty through the neighborhood and often barreled down the steep paved roads, Daddy pumping the brakes and Mac bracing for the bumps, both grinning from ear to ear, wind in their sails, freedom in their souls.

One afternoon, centrifugal force took hold, and off Mac flew like a shot puck, hitting the pavement and rolling like a sausage down the hill. Enter life nine, a much slower, more cautious attempt at being a dog of mature stature.

During the final days of his final life, Mac would hide out in the thick border grass surrounding the azaleas. Since the overgrown shrubbery was taller than he, he was MIA until his raspy cough gave him away, a result of the chicken bones which were lodged in his throat from his younger midnight feasts. Once found, he'd fall out of the bushes, heaving for a breath, eyes bugged, every muscle clenched, refusing, though, to take our pity. Another short week passed, Mac took his last breath, and even Mother the Staunch grieved.

The family will never forgot that dog. Mother and Daddy have since passed away, but the kids and grandkids still remember the promising tenacity Mac had for surviving. He was Mother's bane and Daddy's hope and, in some nostalgic way, our very special memory.

Chapter 8

Intuition:

The act of sensing without the use of rational processes

As if they were our own children, our dogs can spark a knowing in our hearts and souls. Like Santa Claus, we know when they've been sleeping (OK, so we hear them snoring). We know when they're awake (who doesn't? They're in our faces). We know when they've been bad or good (toss a coin). And if we can't say for sure what they're up to, we let our imaginations take over.

In this chapter, named *Intuition*, you'll experience the concern of a mother as she helps her dog Dixie through a long night of illness in "Mama Knows Best." You'll relate to the intuition of a new dog owner as she begins to identify other guardians in "I See Dog People." And you'll weep alongside a black Lab's guardian as she says good-bye to her dear pet in "My Otter."

Our dogs never scoff at our intuition the way our families do. If we're convinced they need to go outside, they go without comment. If we think they need to visit to the vet, they welcome the ride there. When we insist that they aren't feeling well, they wallow in our attention. And we always sense when they need a few extra pats and scratches.

The intense connection we have with our pets is as strong as if we'd borne them ourselves. We welcome experiences that teach us how to fine-tune our intuition, so when scenarios arise, we don't act merely impulsively but oh so heart-and-soulfully.

Paws and Smell the World

Mama Knows Best

by Rebecca Englert

All mothers know what it is like to worry over their babies. Every sneeze or cough, every tummy ache, every bruise or scratch makes us catch our breath in alarm. How can we not? Our love is compacted into these small creatures who belong to us. They depend on us. They can't tell us where they hurt or when they don't feel well, but they don't have to. Oh, yes, mothers always know.

Why is it, then, that some people think it ridiculous when I act out my natural motherly instincts—on my dogs? They are, after all, my children. They may not say "goo-goo," or carry around their Tonka trucks, or have blonde ringlets tied with little pink bows (unless, of course, they're poodles on parade), but they are my babies just the same. I provide them with food, shelter, medical attention, and most of all love. I teach them. I socialize them. I tend to their physical, mental, and emotional

While I cannot claim them on my tax return, they are WORTH EVERY PENNY spent.

needs. I get unlimited joy from them. And while I cannot claim them on my tax return, they are worth every penny spent.

When I become frightened over mishaps with my dogs, the ranges of emotions are predictable. I ponder, I pace, I protect. I peer, I prep, I pity, I pray. I plunge from practical to panic to peaceful. I take pride in being a dog parent—one who is equally as important as any other parent.

Just recently, my youngest dog, Dixie, gave me quite a scare. She had been playing in the yard with my other two dogs. I called them all for dinner, and as soon as they all romped in, Dixie started vomiting. And it happened: split-second panic.

Of course, after the instantaneous pit of panic had passed, I stopped to ponder why a dog can always manage to find the corner of the only rug or floor pillow on which to hurl, even though most of the floor is covered in dog-friendly ceramic tile.

Everyone knows that a dad cannot handle the yucky part of parenting, so naturally Mom is the one who is awarded the duty of cleaning up. So I was temporarily distracted from the overwhelming worry while I started the washer and scrubbed the carpet—a little bit of parental prepping.

As the evening wore on, Dixie continued to be in distress. Eventually, there was nothing left in her stomach. I tried to comfort her by holding her, but she began to shake violently. Protective autopilot popped on. Thoughts of paranoia surfaced; had some sicko given her antifreeze? In a mere two seconds, I was ready to confront and accuse every neighbor I had. I lost all sense of reality. This was a conspiracy! I was ready to charge out the door. Thankfully, my husband talked me out of it. "We have a six-foot privacy fence," he insisted. My shield deflated, and practicality returned.

Soon Dixie begged to go outside. By this time it was very dark and very cold. I couldn't leave my baby out there by herself, especially since she was sick. Like a reconnaissance team, my husband and I, armed with flash-lights, joined Dixie and walked the entire perimeter of the yard looking for anything that might give a clue as to what was wrong with our girl. We didn't see anything suspi-cious. My mind and body pivoted, and we all went back inside.

Dixie beelined it to her crate and lay down. She was pitiful. She kept trying to sleep, but she was quivering so hard, she couldn't get comfortable. I sorted out the many possibilities that screamed at my senses. My conclusion was a frightening plausibility: Dixie was dying.

It was too late at night to take Dixie to the vet. I wanted to crawl in her crate and just hold her. I couldn't quite fit into the small opening though, so my husband and I hunkered down in front of the door and simply looked at her. Amazingly, just our presence comforted her. I was afraid to leave her side because I didn't know if her next breath would be her last. So we all three just lay there, realizing the permanent bond we had. Four agonizing hours we lay, watching her, petting her, hoping for her, rallying for her, praying for her.

Finally, in the wee hours of the morning, Dixie relaxed and fell into a peaceful sleep. My husband and I reluctantly crept to bed a final few hours before dawn, our ears still attuned to her movement.

I don't know what time I fell asleep. When the alarm clock told me it was time to get up, I quickly padded to Dixie's crate, wishing for a miracle. There she sat, happily chewing on her roll of rawhide, looking her usual bouncy self. I whispered a small prayer of thanks, gave a sigh of relief, and dressed for work. I never did figure out what was wrong with her. She has been perfectly fine ever since.

Some people probably think that to stay up watching a dog breathe for hours on end is a ridiculous waste of time. I argue that watching my dogs as a responsible mother helps me breathe easier.

Those folks may also insist that it is "only" a dog. *Only* means solitarily and simply; I have three very complex, very unique dogs who are anything but "only."

Finally, they may say that I am acting out my desire to be a mother. I say what I know: I already am.

Paws and Smell the World

I See Dog People

*'m over forty and a first-time dog owner. And suddenly, everywhere I look, there they are: dog people. Tens upon thousands of them. Shopping at the grocery store. Strolling in the mall. Driving cars. Dining at restaurants. Waiting in line at the movies. A veritable dog people invasion. I love it!

A few months ago, those who I *thought* were dog people used to make me cringe. They were a breed of their own, looking, smelling, and acting different from me. How in the world could they love a *dog*?

Now that I'm one of them, I completely understand the attraction. Dog people are a united front. They're comfortable with dogs and with each other. They're not from another planet, but they often wish non–dog people would leave this one. They're a misunderstood group of individuals who all deserve everyone's respect.

Acquiring the art of seeing dog people can happen overnight and is very similar to spotting the make and model of car you want to buy when you're in the market for a new one. Although you never noticed before, in quite the blink of an eye, 24,000 pewter Chevy Trailblazers line the highways. You probably wonder where they'd all been parked before you took an interest in the model. What you don't realize is that they were there the whole time. You just weren't interested before now. It's the same way with dog people. Now that I have a dog, I see dog people at every corner.

Dog people are actually quite easy to spot. They possess five obvious giveaways: their clothing, their accessories, their personal grooming, their mode of transportation, and, finally, their facial expressions. And under-

Acquiring the art of seeing dog people can happen OVERNIGHT.

standing these five fundamentals can help you determine whether or not you should engage in dog talk, something in which dog people delight.

The clothes that dog people wear are basic. Nothing fussy, nothing dry cleanable, and certainly nothing that picks up lint. Silk is out—too snag prone. They wear a half-size larger than they should for mobility (bending, picking up pup, throwing pup in car) and stick to colors that don't show dog hair. They prefer a comfortable pair of jeans, a T-shirt, and a pair of sneakers over skirts, hose, heels, or ties.

Their accessories are minimal as well. For the women, a simple pair of stud earrings, a short chain-link necklace, a strappy wristwatch, and a ring or two. For men, a wedding ring if they must. Too many bobbles get in the way, can be choking hazards, or can get ripped off during excitable moments. They carry small doggy pictures in their purses or wallets and spend their bucks on novelty items for the dog rather than themselves. In fact, the excess in accessories comes only in the items they buy—you guessed it—for their dogs. Harley Davidson hats, college sweatshirts, and blinking Christmas collars are popular items. And never underestimate the power of a good fashion statement gathered from the canine *Survivor* buff.

Personal grooming can also scream "I'm a dog person!" Again, dog women prefer fast, easy hairstyles, and dog men sport short-cropped cuts. Dog people don't have time for mousse, gel, blow-dryers, curlers, more gel, and hairspray. They're just going to the dog park anyway. Women dog people wear little to no makeup and perfume and avoid long fake nails. But they always smell clean. Dog people like to be clean, and their dogs usually don't stink either.

Dog people have specific modes of transportation, which easily target them as dog drivers. They don't ride the bus or take taxis to work; they own their own sport-utility vehicles and decline the leather seat upgrades upon purchase. They carry an extra towel in the back for muddy tromps in the park. They usually have a few extra leashes, a bottle of water, and a couple of treats tucked away in the glove compartment. Their bumper stickers announce their preferred status in society—DOG may be their copilot, or their Border Collie is probably smarter than your honor roll student. Circular smudges decorate their lower backseat windows, quite obviously from second-row sniffers.

Finally, nonverbal communication says it all. Dog people have a kind look in their eyes. They smile, they laugh, their eyes sparkle, they're excited about life. They look fulfilled. And they are confident. After all, they are dog people, full of purpose and servitude.

Once I began recognizing so many dog people, I felt obliged to take my discoveries one step further. Yes, I've gone live with a failsafe ranking system I call PAWS (Puppy Admirer Wranking System). I've developed degrees within each of the five categories, and with a bit of mathematical precision, voilà! I can give a self-proclaimed dog person the gong or a standing ovation.

For example, my co-worker claims to be a dog person and has vowed that upon retirement, he's going to buy a leash and head straight for the pound for his first adoption.

Right. Ain't gonna happen. How do I know? I use my PAWS. It goes something like this:

Clothing: 3 out of 10. An impeccable dresser—his suits are always pressed, his tie is straight from the cleaners, and a reflection of his shoelaces gleams in his buffed shoes. He wouldn't stand for a dog nudging his calves with a wet nose.

Accessories: Another 3 out of 10. Wears too much jewelry, especially the sea turtle cuff links. A major choking hazard.

Personal Grooming: 8 out of 10. Best personal category. Balding on the top, minimal fussing required. Looks clean, smells clean; however, uses a bit too much aftershave.

Mode of Transportation: 7 out of 10. OK, he passes the SUV test; he's got the Ford Explorer with room in the back for a travel crate. However, the car smells as if it just broke the factory doors. A dog person's car always has a little dog breath in the air and evidence of puppy fluff in the plush.

Facial Expression: 6 out of 10. He looks happy enough, but I see right through that counterfeit smile. He's merely humoring me when we talk about dogs. There's a fear behind that mug that says "I wouldn't know what to do with a dog if I had one. But I'll keep nodding while you tell me about your weekend at the pooch park."

Total Score: 27 out of 50. That's 54 percent, a failing grade in most standards. Uh-uh, no dog person here.

Being a dog person is an admirable thing. It's a great icebreaker at parties, it can force you into extracurricular events like Frisbee-catching competitions and Best in Show galas, and it puts you in a comfortable I-really-fit-in mode, given that there are literally millions of real dog people in the world.

For the first time in my life, I'm able to approach a perfect stranger (who suddenly is not really a stranger at all) and immediately strike up a meaningful conversation about those we have in common—our dogs. I owe all of my newfound bravery to the implicit bond of dog people. Salute!

Paws and Smell the World

My Otter

by Amy Jefferson

Otter, like many black Labs, had quite the vocal repertoire. It was almost as if he could form syllables out of his drawn out bark-growls. "Oooooooouuuuuu," he would say as you drove into the driveway, his body bending back and forth, trying to keep up with his tail. If you didn't know him, you might be afraid. After all, when a ninety-pound animal is charging you, what are you supposed to expect? But, if you had already had the pleasure of an introduction, you'd keep up the conversation. Back and forth, changing pitch and volume, the talking could go on for hours. "Where have you been? There was a squirrel here a minute ago. Do you have any French fries left in that bag? Can we go for a swim later?" The doggy chitchat was never-ending.

While Otter was exceptionally articulate for four-legged

His eyes were ALWAYS there to exchange a comforting glance of understanding.

folk, he spoke even clearer messages with his eyes. Friends would always express their surprise at how his emotions were "worn on his collar." Instead of a growl (one never passed his lips), Otter would simply glower. Instead of a scared whimper, the whites of his eyes would show as he cut them away from whatever was scaring him (usually an armadillo—he wasn't exactly a brave dog). Instead of excited barks, his twinkling eyes would accompany tail wags and kisses.

Otter's eyes twinkled good-morning greetings each day and glared each time I left him behind to run errands. They gave me understanding submission when it was time to lie down. They gave me sparkling yes-yes-yeses when I asked if he wanted to go somewhere. His eyes rolled with mine as we grew together, learning how to live life with a toddler. They cut to the side, ignoring my joking "sic

'em" after animals I knew he'd never pursue. They squinted coyly as he greeted the neighborhood cats he knew he was supposed to hate. But most of all, his eyes were always there to exchange a comforting glance of understanding.

Today, my precious Otter spoke with his eyes for the last time. After a jolting alert from a neighbor, I ran to his side. He had been hit by a car—seriously injured and bleeding badly. Without making a sound, unexpectedly, he greeted me with those talking, twinkling eyes. His tail was wagging through them so clearly as I approached. He could not move, but I know it was wagging. As I lay there and tried to comfort him, he, too, comforted me with his all-knowing eyes and sweet silent talk. When it was time for him to go, he gave me one last look of understanding. A look that said, "I'm sorry . . . I wasn't watching for that car . . . I love you . . . I'll see you again sometime." And without a sound, his eyes closed.

Chapter 9

Responsibility:

The state of being accountable or answerable

From the time we were kids, begging our parents to let us keep the stray, to our role as adults, signing contracts of commitment at the local animal adoption shelter, we have heard the classic line: caring for a dog is a huge responsibility. Breed books emphasize the notion of duty, canine obedience classes begin their sessions with the owner's obligations, and puppy pamphlets italicize the age-old warning. However, the phrase is wrought with truth; responsibility is one of the primary lessons we learn when we take on a dog.

In fact, we learn responsibility from the very moment we become parents of dogs. Whether we are absorbed in potty training, or in bathing and grooming, or in exercising, or in simply loving our new friends, the responsibility concept is larger than life.

This chapter on accountability includes "Daymare at Dog Park," in which a puppy park disaster leads a distraught guardian to rethink the benefits of neutral socialization. One man's best friend—adept at appearing at just the right moments—keeps his owner on

the consciously straight and narrow in "Poppin' Fresh Pup." Finally, the idea that when we are away, dogs will play is underscored in "Pizza Box Blues," a poem that pinpoints how quickly a dangerous and bizarre event can occur.

We have scores of responsibility in this world between our work, our families, our social obligations, and our own personal needs. It's reassuring to know that when the world gets all too overwhelming, the responsibility we owe our dogs immediately comes to the forefront as one of the easiest yet certainly one of the most important jobs we have. Now that's a load off.

Daymare at Dog Park

What a beautiful morning it was to go to his favorite spot: the new thirty-acre Doggie-Wood Park, designed especially for dogs. I knew he loved going to the puppy park because he talked to me with emphatic whimpers the entire drive there. His breathing became shallow and his heart was dancing in his chest from the excitement. He wiggled and waggled until he fell off the backseat onto the floorboard.

Before I could get the car in park, he had jumped into the front seat and was ready to leap from the vehicle to the white rock parking lot. I quickly fastened his leash, grabbed my wallet and keys, and off we raced to the welcome trailer.

The one-visit fee was steep—$10 just to get in. I barely had time to put my change in my wallet before he tugged me out the door and to the entry gate. In ten seconds flat, we were behind the confines of the chain-linked fence, I had unhooked his leash, and he was off like a racehorse, following the other newcomers, sniffing all their tails, making friends, smiling in his own way.

He was in doggy heaven.

What dog wouldn't love this—room to roam, woods for exploring, and a huge lake for cooling off. There were giant sand mounds for digging holes past China, a flat grass lot larger than a football field to sprint after a Frisbee, and large concrete pipes to climb through and find a nice shady spot. Huge aluminum water bowls were located every 200 feet with spigots that spewed cold, clean water. And if you looked really close, you might stumble upon an old tennis ball— yours for throwing and retrieving.

I contemplated either finding a seat at a vacant picnic table, where I could just kick back and watch his every romp, or

He was off like a racehorse, following the other newcomers, sniffing all their tails, making FRIENDS, smiling in his own way.

locating familiar faces so I could casually mingle with other dog parents and gloat about my special dog. I scanned the park and noticed that some very aggressive breeds were present on this day, so I opted for hanging rather close to keep a watchful eye on my dog. After all, he was just a puppy, and I was a somewhat overprotective mom and a wee bit nervous about the new acquaintances he would make.

I whistled and called, encouraging him to sprint toward the lake where the friendly Labs were jumping in and splashing around. But he was distracted by the front gate and the myriad new arrivals and consistently turned back to be part of the welcome waggers.

Afraid that he would bolt through the open entrance gate, I rehooked the leash to his harness and began to drag him toward the party pool. Once I got him to the back of the park, I could relax and let him loose.

No sooner had I connected the leash to his harness, when a large snow-white Akita approached him. The beautiful dog quadrupled mine in size and stature. Both dogs' hair bristled and low growls escaped their mouths. I gave a tug and away we went, down the mulch-lined path, through the woods, closer to where we needed to be.

"This is an off-leash park, lady!" yelled the owner of the Akita.

I glanced back over my shoulder and stood my ground. "I know. I'm just trying to get this little guy to the back of the park. He keeps trying to make a run for the gate."

Another man passed me. "You better unleash him. That's the rule."

I knelt down and released the clip, hoping my puppy would follow me toward the lake. He headed in that direction. My pace slowed. Finally, I could take a deep breath.

But before I knew it, the Akita was there again. Like a white blur, he galloped past me and stopped on top of my dog. More irritated, threatening growls, more frozen stances, then, just as two unneutered males will do, the mating dance began.

My pup wanted no part of this act. A few warning snarls led to a full-on tumbling attack. My dog gripped the neck of the Akita in self-defense but soon let go. I scrambled to secure him with the leash and pulled him back.

"It's the leash, lady. Take him off the leash," the Akita's owner insisted.

"And let your dog attack mine?" I clearly had an attitude at this point. Underneath my bravado, however, was me—timid and compliant. I unhooked my pup.

Before I could stand up straight, the two were at it again, my pup rolling over in submission, the Akita mounting him with pride. Finally, my dog had had enough and attempted to escape. The Akita would not have that. More rumbling ensued and soon a full roll of dust erupted, ending with the Akita clamped to my dog's ear.

Panic shot through my bones. He was just a baby. He was bleeding. I had big plans for him; he was going to be a show dog. The big bully Akita had no right. I had to get him off my dog.

I had valiant intentions, but in the dread, my strength left me, and I was like a limp noodle. The Akita's guardian realized that they were the two who looked foolish now. He bent low and yelled in the ear of his dog. "Let go!" he said. "Let go!'"

Both dogs stood frozen, his feeling superior, gloating; mine full of dignity, not flinching, not blinking, not whimpering, not trying to run like a coward. Blood seeped down the side of his face. I suddenly wished I'd opted to play ball in the backyard.

Instead, I'd paid $10 to watch my dog be mauled.

I did what I knew. I kicked the Akita in the side, over and over, albeit lightly, given that my nerves were shot and I could barely stand from shaking all over. The heated conversation continued.

"Don't kick my dog, lady. I'll sue you."

"Get your dog off my dog, mister, and I'll stop."

"Pull his tail!" someone shouted in our direction.

With weak arms, I tried once, then wised up. The last thing I wanted was the Akita turning on me.

Finally, the dogs separated. The owner of the Akita furiously headed for the front gate, mumbling something about how my dog had attacked his. Some bystanders pulled out a roll of paper towels and offered me a few pieces to wipe the blood from my dog's neck.

The owner of the park found me and suggested that I was smart in letting my pup continue playing with other dogs after the incident. She assured me that the Akita wouldn't be coming back. She suggested I get my dog neutered. She was nervous about the scene I might cause with the media. The park was young and didn't need bad press.

She really didn't know me, though. I was there to give my dog an experience of meeting other dogs. I took my chances, and I knew from the start that just like people, dogs don't always get along. Sometimes things turn sour. That's the price you pay. I'd taken the ultimate chance and was paying for it, but that had been my decision. I couldn't blame the park.

It's been five months since the daymare, and my dog still has a lump beside his ear to remind me of that horrible episode. Luckily, his fur has grown back and has covered the injury, and, as far as I know, he's forgotten about the traumatic episode at Doggie-Wood Park. We even returned a few Saturdays ago, although it didn't hold the allure that it once had.

I'll never place my pup in that situation again. If he needs companionship, we'll play kick ball in the backyard. After all, when was the last time your pup complained about that?

Poppin' Fresh Pup

It's morning. Dull gray light is fighting its way through my curtains, and predawn dreams are holding me down in the bed. I'm Sigourney Weaver in *Aliens*, and I'm about to kill a monster. Up pops the dog in my face. He gives me a soggy new-day lick across my nose. I lose the imaginary battle by drowning in a pool of mucous. I give a raspy snort, open my thick eyelids, and there he is—ready to go out, telling me, "Enough of this slothfulness! Get up. I've got to go potty."

We've been to the dripping-with-dew backyard, and now we're back inside. The won-derful smooth aroma of fresh caramel coffee is finding its way to my nostrils. I pour a cup of the steaming java, plop down in my overstuffed chair, and grab the remote to tune in to the morning news. I pull the mug to my lips and up pops the dog. Hot coffee percolates from my mug onto my

Call him my conscience, my Jiminy Cricket. He keeps me grounded and never lets me forget he's watching my every move and that he is my tremendous RESPONSIBILITY..

nose, and my shoulders shake in response to the burning pain. "I'm thirsty, too, you know," he gripes. "And some food wouldn't hurt, either."

I move to the computer to check my e-mail, a habit that helps me wake up. I'm reading a reply from my agent, something unusually positive about the publisher who liked my latest submission and might consider it with a few changes. I open the document and work for a while on the wording. I press the mouse to prepare to save and up pops the dog. The cursor jumps from Yes to No and the newly composed brilliance is lost. "You sit in front of that screen too much," he chastises me. "There's a whole world out there, you know."

I throw on some old sweats and lace up my running shoes. I'm off for the beach to get in a few miles before the summer crowds gather. I slip into my VW Bug, and before I can get the keys in the ignition and the door closed, up pops the dog. "Where do you think you're going?" he interrogates. "Trying to escape, huh? Slide over. I'm coming, too."

I'm winded now after putting in a satisfying three kilometers on the hard-packed sand. The sun is warm on my shoulders, and I drop to the ground to catch my breath and watch the waves. I lie back, hands behind my head, and close my eyes to see if I can continue the morning's earlier action dream. Up pops the dog, sand flying in every direction, his heavy panting overpowering the crashing surf. He steps on my stomach and pauses, as if he's just conquered a beached whale. "I'm done with this place," he announces. "I've chased all the seagulls I'm going to chase. They've flown the coop, and I'm pooped. Take me home."

I grab a sub from the sandwich shop on the way back to the house. It's a challenge to steer, change gears, and eat all at once, but I can do it if I concentrate. I take a bite at the stoplight, and up pops the dog who bumps my elbow. Tomatoes, bell peppers, and lettuce explode onto my lap, and he looks away, disgusted, and sighs indignantly. "Well, that wasn't worth the effort," he complains. "You vegetarians just kill me."

My life would be very lonely without my companion. Call him my conscience, my Jiminy Cricket. He keeps me grounded and never lets me forget he's watching my every move and that he is my tremendous responsibility. The way I figure, life needs a few surprises. And who better to give them than a poppin' fresh pup.

Pizza Box Blues

by Laura Kangas

Lacy liked her big backyard.
Squirrel smells made her day.
But that all changed a week ago
When trouble came her way.

She was mindin' her business,
chewin' a bone,
When suddenly she got a whiff:
A well-known smell of sausage and
cheese—
Her favorite stuff to sniff!

She was all alone; the time was right,
And there within Lacy's reach

Beware of the words *REFORM SCHOOL!*

Was a pizza box with one last slice,
Tempting her to nab a piece.

Her dad was gone, so she strolled
to the stove
And lunged toward the oven door.
Her nose aligned with the top of the range.
Her back feet were still on the floor.

With one quick swipe she finally had
Within her trembling jaws,
Meat and cheese and chewy crust,
Helped to her mouth by her paws.

Alpo was Lacy's favorite food.
It tasted like turkey stew.
But gobbling this pizza's spicy sauce,
Made her bark, "And here's to you!"

On her way back down to the wooden
planks,
Lacy made one mistake:
Her right front paw ignited the gas;
That pizza box sealed her fate.

Next thing she knew the firemen came,
And someone phoned Lacy's dad
Who burst through the door and

then gave her that look—
That look that he gets when he's mad.

She said she was sorry and hung her
head low,
But now there was one big mess.
A thousand bucks later and a bunch of
smoke
Had caused tremendous distress.

The moral of the story is one to heed
For a dog who ignores the rule:
Before you sneak a leftover snack,
Beware of the words *reform school*!

Chapter 10

Inclusion:

The state of belonging to a group

We all want to belong. Whether we admit it or not, we desire to be part of a group that shares commonalities. We are comforted by similar beliefs and actions. We find solace in knowing we are not alone in our convictions. We enjoy the conversations we have with others who feel the same way we do. We like to say with satisfied surprise, "Me, *too*!"

This chapter, titled *Inclusion*, drives home the idea that while we may not realize that we have a passion to belong, it often overtakes our every decision and explains why we behave the way we do.

In "I Have a Dog," one lady searches for two decades before she understands that canine parenting is not about suddenly "owning" a dog—it's about a lifetime of "owing" a dog that which you've promised him. Join Annie, one party-going pup whose reputation as a howling hound makes some wonder if she's gone to the dogs in the whimsical poem "That Gal Can Howl." And in "Grand Theft Frodo," a pair of wannabe grandparents' wish comes true when their daughter adopts a new baby—er, puppy.

People who choose to complete their lives with the addition of dogs as companions can rest assured that they fall into a very large group, for, astounding as it may seem, dogs reside in well over 40 million households. Enjoy this chapter, and know that you'll definitely never walk alone.

Paws and Smell the World

I Have a Dog

I once had the cycle of dog ownership all wrong. I wanted a dog so I could be like everybody else. I wanted a dog so I could be included in that elite group of doggers. I wanted a dog because it seemed like the right thing to do. That's why it never worked for me. It took twenty years to finally get it right, and boy did I get it right this time. Take a look at the progression:

We lived in a rental unit on the historical posh side of town. I was a newlywed, childless, with a husband who loved sailing on his boat with friends more than shopping in the mall with me. I was a teacher with summers off, so I had to be creative to fully occupy my three months of free time. I figured a new puppy would do the trick. Enter Niblet. He was the most precious black-and-white Boston Terrier on earth, and his markings in- dictated he would be a

It took three wrong tries and twenty years to find the PERFECT FIT, but it was worth the wait.

champ. A little food, a little water, a few strokes on his soft fur, and I'd raise this puppy with no problems. Or so I thought.

By the second week, I was pulling my hair out. Niblet wanted no part of the cardboard box hotel that we placed in our bedroom closet. Each night he'd scratch and squeal until I gave in, and come four in the morning, I was huddled on the living room couch watching Niblet circle the carpet, ready to play. Sleep deprived and irritable, I handed Niblet back to my mother-in-law with a heavy but realistic heart. I wasn't ready.

Seven years later I tried it again. I had two young sons who needed a good dog. I had a house with a big backyard. The setting and timing were perfect. I couldn't lose.

"You just need the right dog this time," encouraged my husband. "A German Shepherd Dog would be perfect." He suggested we visit the pound to select a dog that wasn't purebred and as difficult as Niblet.

The attendant added her two cents. "You want a dog that's seen the ropes, not a fragile puppy. Besides, this one is hearty and can live outside." I nodded, excited that I didn't have to keep the dog in my bedroom closet at night. I might be able to maintain my sleep habits.

Sasha the Shepherd came home with us that day. She was the usual brown with black around the tips of her perky ears, pointed muzzle and thick tail, and although she was bigger than the boys, she was easy with them.

She lasted three months. She chewed up the garden hose, my husband's running shoes, the gardenia bushes, and my children's yard toys. She had a horrible habit of pooping right outside the door rather than at the back of the lot, and she barked incessantly at the moon. A great family in the country took her in, and she spent the rest of her days on their five-acre grounds with their horse.

As if I hadn't learned my lesson, I did it again. I decided my now preteen sons could help with the raising of a dog—it would be a good experience for them. All their friends had dogs—why shouldn't they?

I was convinced that I merely needed a puppy whose personality fit the neighborhood. We had just moved into a large new home, and I needed a housedog who didn't mind being alone during the day and who could be trained to walk on a leash around the neighborhood in the evenings. We'd be the "in" couple with the beautiful Boxer named Roxy. This was my worst mistake yet.

We picked Roxy from a large litter of pups. She was the frisky one—a sign of health, my husband insisted. She snuggled with my sons in the backseat of the car on the way home. Upon entering the house, she promptly peed in the foyer and never stopped peeing on the Berber carpet until the day we said good-bye to her. When visitors would arrive, we'd open the front door and whoosh! Roxy was off—not to greet the guests, but to race down the street until she was out of sight. She grew bigger than the crazy look in her eyes, and we began to suspect that she was inbred.

An advertisement went into the paper, and for minimum return on our investment, a nice couple took Roxy to their country home where she bred her own litters of crazy pups.

I was finished. No more dogs for this family. Or so I thought. I remembered my husband telling stories about the old dog from the gym where he used to work. If I wanted a good dog, he advised, an English Bulldog would do the trick. But, he warned, he'd have no part in raising this dog. I was on my own.

I decided I wouldn't rush out and pick the first puppy I saw. I bought a stuffed version of the dog I wanted, so I could get used to having a furry friend around the house. I conducted months of research over the Internet, searching for the perfect pup with the perfect look. Finally, I found him. An imported fawn and white bully pup ready to go.

His Lithuanian lineage was long. With a father named Mervander Thundervoice, a strong sturdy Bulldog with countless championship titles in Russian dog shows, I felt sure I had picked a winner. Armis Perkunkimis was his given name. Needless to say, we would find another one.

My drive to Tennessee and back with my two sons proved rewarding the moment we cuddled our new baby. We decided on the new name during the drive home, tossing out insulting titles like T-Bone and Winston and choosing instead the more appropriate name *Dozer*. Fittingly, he slept the whole way.

Dozer is now part of our tribe. We've conquered potty training, taught him tricks, and consider him the personality that completes our family. It took three wrong tries and twenty years to find the perfect fit, but it was worth the wait. With pride I can say I really do have a dog.

Paws and Smell the World

That Gal Can Howl

Annie, it's a full round moon.
The time is right; it's nearly June.
We're gathered 'round to hear you croon.

How that gal can howl.

We'll work you up a roaring fire.
Have a treat and get inspired.
Be our twelve o' clock town crier.

How that gal can howl.

Lift your muzzle; pitch your voice.
Your entertainment is quite choice.
Listen to that unique noise.

How that gal can howl.
Ooooooohhhhh, Oooooooooh!

Take a breath and let it rip.
Send us on a canine trip.
No rehearsal, no set script.

How that gal can howl.

Witness this amazing feat.
Annie is so kind and sweet.
Louder than a sheep's last bleat.

How that gal can howl.

She's the envy of the crowd.
When howls escape her lips, we're wowed.
No dog could ever be so proud.

How that gal can howl.
Ooooooohhhhh, Oooooooooh!

I hope you don't misunderstand.
Those moments—they were never
planned.

Bark up a STORM; just come unglued.

They're not part of a scheme so grand.

How that gal would howl.

In conversation, we'd all be.
The wind would pick up through
the trees.
Her nerve would ride in on the breeze.

How that gal would howl.

The clouds would part; the stars
would shine.
One minute she'd be rightly fine.
Then one too many treats divine,

How that gal would howl.
Ooooooohhhhh, Oooooooooh!

Sitting in the pitch-black dark,
Singing like a meadowlark,
One note morphed into a bark.

How that gal did howl.

The bark went dry; she tried again.
Her voice cracked to our chagrin.

She took another biscuit in.
How that gal did howl.

Trying hard to gain control,
The howl came pouring from her soul.
Though that wasn't quite her goal,

How that gal did howl.
Ooooooohhhhh, Oooooooooh!

We had to curb our evening fun.
All dogs were howling, on the run.
They came in packs in search of one.

Where's that gal who howled?

Soon a noise ordinance was born.
Anne was banned from tootin' her horn.
That made Annie so forlorn.

Where's that gal who howled?

But on occasion she does flip.
Not wanting to be a social drip.
She blames it on a vocal slip.

How that gal can howl.
Ooooooohhhhh, Oooooooooh,
Ooooooohhh, Ooooooohhh!

So when you're feeling rather blue
You know what you need to do.
Bark up a storm; just come unglued.

Drop your jowl and howl!

Grand Theft Frodo

by Laura Kangas

I am a thirty-six-year-old woman—really much closer to thirty-seven than thirty-six. From the time I was seventeen years old, I began to assume that I would eventually *want* to get married and *want* to have children. The years continued to tick by, and while my interest in being married was always *vaguely* present, my desire and interest in birthing children to produce a grandchild for my parents was all but nonexistent.

My parents, who are in their mid-seventies, already have one grandchild, thanks to my older brother, and they are truly fulfilled by that relationship. But he is fifteen years old now and over six feet tall; hard to cuddle and hold in your lap. Little did we all know that my parents' long-dormant desire to be grand-parents, yet again, to a warm, affectionate, and eternally small being would soon be satisfied.

I've discovered that this four-legged infant has them completely SMITTEN.

On a cold day in December, we were blessed.

We were blessed with the arrival of a very small baby Chihuahua whom I named Frodo. After already raising two other dogs over the past seven years, I was somewhat hesitant to take on the role of new "mom" once more. My trepidation was completely erased once I held out my hands to greet the squirming black-and-tan bundle of joy. He weighed one-and-a-half pounds upon the first intro-duction to our small household. The mother dog had weaned the pups early, so they had to be sent to new homes as soon as possible. I hurried to the store and bought a soft blue (since he is a boy) receiving blanket. I held the coverlet around my neck during the thirty minute drive to meet him (to be sure it would pick up my scent) so that he would recognize me as *his mother*. And so it happened: I had produced a grandchild.

I brought my new baby home and settled him in. Summoning all my fortitude and past dog experience, I immediately set out to accomplish the expected dog-mother tasks of loving, training, and house-breaking. I wholeheartedly accepted this responsibility just as I had with my other two dogs, expecting no help from outsiders. After all, I *am* the parent, and I will bear the burden. That is, unless there are grandparents.

Grandparents are an odd lot. While they *never* want to intrude, they do want to *help*. As parents, we gladly accept their help on occasion; they call it help, I call it *theft*. Despite the grandparental cover-up, I've discovered that this four-legged infant has them completely smitten. His simple presence alone can (and does) completely make their day, and their obsession with stealing him away is borderline (albeit healthy) neuroticism. Their desire to act as his caretaker was subtle at first. Yes, I saw it coming, but I gave in:

Grandparent: "He's awfully small. Do you *really* think you should leave him home alone all day?"

Parent: "Yes, he's fine. He has to learn to be independent and feel secure on his own."

Grandparent: "Maybe we should just come and get him; we'll keep him for you during the day, until he gets a little bigger."

Parent: "Alright . . . BUT, you don't have to do this *every* day."

Grandparent: "Oh, we won't; just days when we aren't too busy."

Fast-forward three years. We've all settled into our daily roles quite nicely.

The "grand-dog" (as he is now known) usually goes to "Gammaw's and Gang-Gang's" every single day while we are at work. The "grandfather" drives approximately one-and-a-half miles most mornings at approximately eight o'clock to pick up the "grand-dog." The daily ceremony of pick up and delivery culminates with a celebratory greeting, delicious treats, special (favorite) toys, and even a routine strangely reminiscent of that of any four-year-old child once "Gammaw" takes over. As the dutiful parent, I arrive each afternoon to pick up the "grand-dog" on my way home from work. The obligatory parental afternoon banter rallies with questions and answers about the baby's day:

Parent: "How did he do today?"

Grandparent: "Oh, Frodo was fine. He did play in the backyard quite a while, but then he came inside and took a nap for probably two hours!"

Parent: "Good. He hasn't been sleeping much lately, and I know he needed to catch up on his rest."

Grandparent: "Oh, and he didn't eat much. We put his food out for him, but he didn't seem hungry. Maybe he will eat tonight."

Parent: "That's fine. I'm sure he's all right and will eat when he's really hungry."

And so, my (still) nonexistent desire to be the mother of any human children has been forever replaced and satisfied by my role as the mother of an eight-pound three-year-old covered in black-and-tan fur. My parents' desire to be grandparents once again and impart their seventy-plus years of loving wisdom has been fulfilled. Their need for that something or "someone" to make them feel needed and, better yet, included once again as an influential part of a small, growing life has been met. Except this time, there is no six-foot tall man-child to reckon with; only a small, trusting, completely dependent, four-legged soul.

I have come to believe that the gift I gave my parents as an afterthought has now found a more significant meaning and purpose for us all. It is proudly displayed this very day on the back bumper of the grandparents' vehicle. With bright red backing and large white letters for all to read, it says:

Ask Me About My Granddog!

Paws and Smell the World

A crisp morning dew on a still early light;
It rides on the wind from its trip through
the night.
It tickles my senses, and try as I might,
I can't make you stop and take note.

The sun burns the mist, and the day
stands tall.
The oak trees insist that their leaves
must fall.
The grass is their blanket, and it cradles
them all,
But I can't make you stop and enjoy.

Give me time; let's take it slowly.
Give me love, and I won't be lonely.
I can teach you if you'd only
Paws and smell the world.

The afternoon wrinkles. The day takes a bow.
The sun fades behind a gray patch of clouds.
If I could speak these words, I'd bellow
out loud:
Paws and smell the world.

The stars dot the sky like a white clover field.
The darkness is heavy and the dampness
surreal.
I just hope that someday your soul
becomes healed.

It will if you stop and breathe deep.
Oh, oh, breathe.
Oh, oh, breathe.

Give me time; let's take it slowly.
Give me love, and I won't be lonely.
I can teach you if you'd only
Paws and smell the world.
Paws and smell the world.

The afternoon wrinkles. The day takes a
bow.
The sun fades behind a gray patch of clouds,
And if I could speak these words, I'd bellow
out loud:

Paws and Smell the World.
Paws and Smell the World.
Paws and Smell the World.

*(Set to music by Derrick Jefferson [a.k.a. Ace Winn]; song
can be heard at* www.drdanathomas.com.)